CARRY A CHICKEN IN YOUR LAP

CARRY A CHICKEN IN YOUR LAP

IN YOUR LAP

Or Whatever It Takes to
Globalize Your Business

Bruce Alan Johnson
and R. William Ayres

ST. MARTIN'S PRESS ❈ NEW YORK

www.stmartins.com

Book design by Phil Mazzone

Library of Congress Cataloging-in-Publication Data

Johnson, Bruce Alan.
  Carry a chicken in your lap : or whatever it takes to globalize your business / Bruce Alan Johnson and R. William Ayres. — 1st ed.
      p. cm.
  Includes index.
  ISBN 978-0-312-56553-4
  1. International business enterprises—Personnel management.
2. International business enterprises—Employees.   3. Employee selection.
4. Employment in foreign countries.   I. Ayres, R. William.   II. Title.
  HF5549.5.E45J64 2009
  658.3—dc22

                                                            2009019931

First Edition: November 2009

10 9 8 7 6 5 4 3 2 1

For Alan G. Finkel
A better friend—and boss—is not to be found

Contents

This chapter leads off with a gripping example—witnessed personally by one of the authors—of an international assignment gone horribly wrong. The story illustrates the basic problem: companies often set themselves up for failure by sending the wrong people to the wrong places, with the wrong expectations. Building on this example, this chapter outlines the problem—selecting personnel and setting them up for success—and gives an overview of the rest of the book, with signposts to guide the reader.

2. Why Go Overseas?   8

Taking your organization overseas may sound like a lot of trouble.
If it's so difficult to get this right, why bother? We argue that taking
your organization international is no longer optional. Current economic circumstances and long-term trends dictate that American
and Canadian companies broaden their horizons. This chapter deals
with issues of shrinking domestic markets, changing currency values, and the future of opportunity—for individuals as well as companies.

3. I'm Not a Racist!   22

This chapter takes on the big issues—gender, race, and religion. The
authors show how characteristics that are too politically correct to
touch in the United States dictate who can be effective and who can't
overseas: American blacks in South Africa, women in Saudi Arabia or
running an office in Dubai. We also deal with family issues—are potential expats married? Do they have children? There's an old wise
saying: "If Momma ain't happy, ain't nobody happy." This chapter
deals with these selection problems head-on, so businesses don't have
to fail because they didn't ask "sensitive" questions.

4. It's Not Just What You Say—It's How You Say It   38

A host of communication skills and abilities are needed for international success. The ability to learn a foreign language is obviously one. (We know a man who once attempted to thank a former
head of state in his own language, but all he could get out was "Buy
a burrito!") But communication is more than language—it's cultural sensitivity, which is sensitivity to meaning. If you can't think
in terms of hidden, symbolic, or cultural meanings (as a U.S. celebrity discovered in a flap over a Maoist handbag in Peru), you don't
belong overseas. This chapter uses stories to illustrate key points
about communication abilities, and how to identify and select people
who have them.

5. No Missionaries!

Beyond the characteristics of the people sent overseas and their symbolic meanings (sending women to Saudi Arabia, for example), companies need to be careful about sending individuals who have an agenda to Change the World. Well-meaning businesses and individuals can get caught up in trying to "fix" everything about a host country. Employees—*and their spouses*—must stay out of the host country's affairs. As William James points out, we have to take the world as it is, not how it ought to be or how we would like it to be. If success is solving all the world's problems, you've already failed. This is not to discourage dreaming big, but dreams without grounding in reality are simply hallucinations.

6. It's 8 AM Somewhere

People who can't adapt to thinking in multiple time zones have no business being sent overseas. Time flexibility is key—and probably can't be taught. But businesses also need to deal with unrealistic expectations of their employees. Humans can't work in two extreme time zones in the same day; companies can't call at 3 AM just because it's convenient for Oshkosh. We face biological absolutes when dealing across time zones. People *do* need to sleep, and 24-7 doesn't work for an individual human. Finally, time is thought about differently (sometimes *very* differently) by each culture. Illustrated with stories across a variety of cultures, this chapter makes key points about setting employees up for success instead of undermining them with unrealistic expectations.

7. I Can't Ask *That*!

Connected to the "I'm Not a Racist" chapter, this chapter talks about constraints on getting the information you need about your employees. It's tough—but necessary, within legal constraints—to have honest conversations about religion, family, and other personal subjects. Companies need to gather information through fair and open information-sharing between employee and company that *respects* the rights of both. Not gathering this information is *not* an option just because it's a "prickly issue." Here's how to effectively handle that process.

8. But It's My Turn!   95

Overseas assignments are often made for foolish bureaucratic and political reasons—because it's "Fred's turn" or because he's somebody's cousin or because she's being punished for something unrelated. (Or, arguably worse—and we've actually heard this voiced—"He succeeded wonderfully in Oshkosh, so he has to succeed in Oslo!") Picking your overseas managers this way is a quick road to failure. Likewise, sending people overseas because it's part of a larger "development track" for all management employees is a good way to guarantee a number of disasters. This chapter will examine the bureaucratic forces behind choosing expats for reasons other than their likelihood of success.

9. In the Imperial Orbit   104

With apologies to our Canadian readers, being an *American* company in a world that has, to a great extent, been structured by U.S. power creates special issues. The United States may be the "sole remaining superpower," but this should *not* be confused with omnipotence, or freedom from consequences for U.S. companies if they mess up. Being American does not protect you from the follies of your mistakes. American law does not extend beyond American shores. But being an American *does* mean foreigners have certain beliefs—and suspicions—about you and your company, regardless of how you see yourself. Many people around the world fear America—for good reason. You have to deal with that and build good relationships in spite of it. If your potential partners think you're a cat's-paw for U.S. policy, you're dead in the water. If you do business with the U.S. government, you may in fact *be* an instrument of U.S. policy—which may not be in your business's best interests, either. This chapter addresses this issue as well.

Your people will have partners overseas. These partners must be as carefully selected as the people you send abroad. Knowing whom to trust and who can be relied on takes a *lot* of background work. *And* it takes money—you cannot get good local partners for free, so don't try to do this on the cheap. "You get what you pay for" doesn't end at the water's edge. Few people are qualified to judge agents, reps, or partners in foreign lands. Yet many companies foolishly expect their overseas candidates to do exactly that. Finding foreign partners you can trust is a key to success. We lay out the fundamentals in this chapter and point you in the right direction for finding the help you need.

Too many companies operate on the precipice of the Foreign Corrupt Practices Act. Messing this up can bring employees back for prosecution and bring disrepute to the company and its efforts. There is a difference between bribery and facilitation; if you don't understand that distinction, the people you send overseas can land in real trouble, fast. This is partly a legal issue and partly an issue of cultural respect. Failing to account for both can lead to disaster. We explain it all here.

What do you do if *you* want to be sent overseas? Not everybody can or should go on overseas assignments, but if you have the essential requirements, you can make yourself more valuable to your company as an expat. This chapter will cover the critical first step—honest self-assessment. You owe it to yourself and your employer to know your strengths and weaknesses before you try to get yourself sent overseas.

13. I've Got What It Takes—Now What?   **161**

Assuming you have done your homework from the previous chapter and are convinced you *are* the right person to go overseas—what now? This chapter discusses skills and knowledge you can develop ahead of time to make yourself more successful as an expatriate, and to pitch yourself to your employer as the right person for the job.

14. Start with the Basics and Get It Right   **168**

This conclusion brings the book together. Go back to the basics—whom do you send? If someone can't adapt, don't send him. Don't choose people for stupid reasons—think it through. Focus on what you expect that person to contribute, not on wishful thinking or imagination. Pick the right person and get results!

Acknowledgments

We first began talking about this book several years ago, when Bruce still lived in South Africa and Bill was still in Indianapolis. Since then, we've both moved (Bruce back to Vermont in the USA, Bill to a different state) and taken on new and different projects. But the book has been a constant thread throughout all the other changes.

It is impossible, of course, to write a book without piling up debts to various people who help you along the way. It is even more so when *two* authors are involved, because both of us consulted with and enlisted the aid of various people. While there's always the danger of forgetting and leaving someone out, we'd like to thank as many of these people as we can for the support and aid they've given us.

A sounding-board role is never an easy appreciated one, but Professor Antoine L. van Gelder (Head of Internal Medicine at the University of Pretoria in South Africa and a world expert on the Eli Goldratt management tool, The Theory of Constraints) listened with stoic patience to Bruce in South Africa, as this book slowly took shape. His counterpoints and wise thoughts helped this book immensely. Alan G. Finkel, retired senior leader of the world conglomerate ITT, worked from a platform of simple integrity and a storehouse of wisdom he himself often does not realize he has. His listening—and even a few of his nits—enriched this book. Finally, if this book receives any praise for content and attention to detail, the credit belongs to Deidre McCoy Berkopes, who heads research for our company. Her remarkable skills have left many senior executives in awe. In our own opinion, there is no more consummate professional in research alive.

Bill owes a debt of gratitude to many of his former colleagues at the University of Indianapolis for supporting his very unacademic habit of sticking his nose into new corners and exploring new ideas. Particularly helpful were Kathy Bohley, for inviting him into the business tent in the first place, and Larry Sondhaus and David Anderson, who supported most if not all of his entrepreneurial ideas for going off in new directions. Special thanks to my colleagues in international relations, Jyotika Saksena and Milind Thakar, for many long and interesting conversations, and to Jim Fuller for being an outstanding colleague.

At Elizabethtown College, Bill would like to thank the Business Department, and Sean Melvin in particular, for being kind enough to invite him in and giving him the opportunity to teach business students. Thanks also to Hossein Varamini, Sanjay Paul, and Petru Sandu, with whom he has had many excellent conversations about things both business-related and international.

Finally, Bill wants to thank his wife Susan, who has the patience of a saint and a heart of gold.

Together, we owe a great deal to three people without whom this book would not have been possible. Our agent, Sammie Justesen, who (along with her husband Dee) understood what we were trying to do almost immediately, got behind us, and has given us tremendous backing. And our editor, Phil Revzin at St. Martin's Press and his assistant editor Kylah Goodfellow McNeill, kindred spirits in many ways, have been patient and helpful throughout. Both Sammie and Phil contributed ideas and stories, some of which we even listened to! Trite as it is to say it, without them the book you are holding would not exist, and for that—and for their friendship and support—we are eternally grateful.

Preface

A television program, about to show some remarkable feat of skill and daring, intones: "Kids, don't try this at home."

Across the bottom of the screen of a car commercial, as the car careens sideways across a road with tires spinning and smoking, the message scrolls: "Closed Course. Professional Driver. Do Not Attempt."

Nearly every appliance, from small clock radios to refrigerators and washing machines, has a box on it somewhere that reads: "Caution: Risk of Electric Shock. Do Not Open. No Parts Fixable by User."

We don't even notice these little reminders. They are part of the background noise of our lives. But why are they there? Why do we need to tell ourselves not to do things that we obviously shouldn't do?

We can easily point the finger at lawyers (it's to keep from getting sued), lax parents (if people would only raise their kids right), or the fact that there's always somebody ready to do something manifestly stupid. But really, these messages are there for all of us. Because deep in our culture, we believe something that unfortunately turns out to be wrong much of the time: *anybody can do anything, if they just try hard enough.*

Of course, we know this isn't true in a lot of areas. Very few of us try to fix our own cars—and those that do spend a lot of time learning how to do it first. We don't try to perform medical procedures on our family members. Most of the time we don't even give them haircuts. There are many things that we're perfectly willing to leave to the professionals.

But this underlying belief runs deep nonetheless. At one time or another, many of us have walked through a modern art museum and thought, "Geez, I could do *that.*" People are constantly bombarding publishers and writers' agents begging to write books, when it's clear they probably shouldn't (hopefully, by the end of this book you won't put us in that category!). And the conversations we hear every day are filled with opinions about how to run the country, how to fix the economy, or how to do somebody else's job better than they can. We do this because, somewhere deep inside us, we believe that *we really could—how hard could it be?*

This is a book about one arena—the world of international business—where people make this mistake all the time. And while we have a number of themes and ideas, this is one of the most important: in international business, *not everybody can do this.*

Yes, anybody can buy a plane ticket and go to Tokyo to have a meeting. Anybody (and in our experience, we do mean *anybody*) can get a job as a vice president of International Operations or director of Overseas Manufacturing or what have you. And anybody can get posted to the overseas branch of the company. People can and do get these jobs all the time, and many of them fail.

What we're trying to say with this book is, *not just anybody* can do these things and succeed. Some people can, and some can't. In other words, in international business our deep-seated belief that anybody can do anything if they just put their mind to it doesn't apply. We want you to start thinking of international operations more like brain surgery, and less like writing a letter. Anybody can learn to write a letter. Not everyone can be successful in the international arena.

This is true in large part because while the world is full of differences, much of the world is not very tolerant of those differences. This is something that can be hard for Americans and Canadians to understand, because we are raised to value differences and diversity. But much of the world thinks differently.

We are reminded of this on a weekly basis. This book is filled with stories—from our own experiences, from our friends and associates, and from others' (often well-publicized) mistakes. New ones come along all the time. After the text of the book was finished, we came across another story—a young British woman in one of the small Persian Gulf states, arrested and jailed on the accusation of having an affair with her boss. She was made to sign a confession in Arabic that she did not understand, and her "hearing" was a mere fifteen minutes long, also in Arabic. Was this unfair? To our eyes, absolutely. But that is the reality of conservative Muslim cultures: young, single, Western women will find it very difficult, even impossible, to be effective there.

On the other hand, there are people who move very well across borders. They can learn languages, adapt to new customs, translate across time zones, and find acceptance among partners and peers in very different parts of the world. They can succeed, wherever they go and whatever it takes to succeed there—even if it means putting on a business suit and riding fifty miles into the countryside with a chicken on their lap.

This book isn't a critique of the rest of the world, or of Canadian or American ways of doing business. As you'll see through the stories we tell, sometimes North Americans are right, and sometimes our hosts and partners overseas are right. We aren't all that interested in who's right and who's wrong. We're interested in, as Peter Drucker put it, *effectiveness*—getting the right things done internationally.

And speaking of effectiveness, as this preface goes to press, the United States government has launched a surprisingly aggressive campaign against American companies operating overseas, rooting out suspected violations of the powerful Foreign Corrupt Practices Act, which we lay out for you clearly in Chapter 11. Do please take that chapter very seriously, because we assure you that any violations of that law will be committed on the overseas end—by the people you send overseas. *Once again, the key will be whom you choose to send overseas!*

What follows from this is a concern with two things: how do you *pick the right people* to send overseas, and how do you *set them up for success*? This book is about both, although we lean most heavily on the first question, because it's been largely ignored by everybody—mostly because international business is one of those areas that looks deceptively simple. Most of the time, we really do think that anybody can do international business well. And we're wrong.

Whether you're just starting out or have been in the international arena for years, we hope your organization has tremendous success in globalizing itself. We hope the stories and points made in this book can help. But mostly, we hope that you find the right people and take the right chances—even if, as one of us did, you have to carry a chicken on your lap to do it—to get the right things done around the world.

CARRY A CHICKEN IN YOUR LAP

1

Failure Before You Even Start

"NO WAY!" SHE SHOUTED at the top of her lungs. "You're not getting that damned thing on me!"

She was a young American woman, perhaps in her midtwenties. The "thing" was a black cloth *chador,* the modesty garment worn by Muslim women throughout most of the Islamic world. The place was inside a Boeing 747 commercial aircraft about half an hour out from the airport of a major Arab country.

The crew tried calmly to tell the upset woman that passing out such garments to Western women before landing was required by national law. But she would have none of it. "You'll be arrested, miss, and probably treated very harshly," the *maître de cabine* warned her in soft tones. "Because not to be covered modestly and properly is considered to be an offense unto Allah."

All to no avail. After we landed, a heated exchange in Arabic with security police took place at the forward door of the aircraft. Seconds later three officers yanked the woman from her seat and dragged her yelling down the ramp connected to the plane. Bruce was not far behind them, hoping he might help. But it was too late. A representative of the dreaded religious police, or *muta'awa,* was now joining the party. He lashed at the woman's exposed legs with a small whip, inducing cries and tears.

Within a few hours, she had been arrested, released, and placed against her will onto an aircraft destined for a European city.

Bruce pursued the story. She was a middle-management employee of a large American multinational corporation, on her first overseas assignment. She had been given almost no training whatsoever for entering an Arab country that was highly orthodox in its observance of the strictures of Islam.

She was the wrong person, sent by a company that had not done its homework, to a country whose environment and realities had been completely disregarded.

It was a disaster, but one that could so easily have been prevented.

For a lot of reasons—all of them wrong, as we explain in this book—too many American and Canadian companies assume that anyone on their staffs can succeed overseas. As you just read, this is a wrong assumption—usually, in our considerable experience, a catastrophic one. And it is a very, very expensive assumption.

THE COSTS OF SENDING THE WRONG PEOPLE

Every year American corporations send thousands of employees overseas. Sadly, around 75 percent of them fail. Since it costs roughly $300,000 a year to maintain an employee overseas, and the average assignment runs four years, this means they are spending $1.2 million per employee sent abroad. With an aggregated 75 percent failure rate, this means that companies are investing the equivalent of $1.2 million with a 75 percent chance of getting little or nothing back. Or, put another way, *they are losing roughly*

$3.5 million out of every $5 million invested in sending people overseas! It has been estimated that *American firms alone lose $2 billion per year in direct costs because of sending the wrong people overseas.*

Wow. Huge losses. But, even worse, many ruined lives. All of it is completely avoidable, but little understood. Because we believe that the success rate can be improved through learning new principles, we've written this book.

TO OUR CANADIAN FRIENDS . . .

If you're a Canadian reading this book, the figures above might induce a small sense of smug self-satisfaction. "Those Americans," you might say. "They have never been any good at paying attention to the rest of the world. We here in Canada—we know better. We speak more than one language. We're not nearly so arrogant. We know how to do this."

We wish heartily that this were true. If it were, this book would be filled with Canadian success stories to contrast with American failures. But the truth is, while both sides of the border have had some successes, both have had a tremendous number of failures as well—and usually for the same reasons. We are indebted to Canadian journalist Andrea Mandel-Campbell and her work, especially her recent book *Why Mexicans Don't Drink Molson: Rescuing Canadian Business from the Suds of Global Obscurity*, in which she catalogs those errors far more thoroughly than we can. Don't take our word for it; take hers. And remember that only fifty companies in Canada account for half your country's exports. (A couple of quotes from Andrea's book worth pondering: "Given what Canadians have been able to achieve at home, in such a harsh and unforgiving climate, going abroad is eminently doable. If we can build ice roads across hundreds of kilometres of barren, treeless tundra that are able to withstand the merciless pounding of thousands of transport trucks as they make their way to Yellowknife . . . just south of the Arctic Circle, then we can do anything. It's a matter of first *wanting to*, and then familiarizing ourselves with the new topography." But: "In fact, most [Canadian] SMEs [small-to-medium-size enterprises] do not even *think* about exporting. According to a poll taken by the Canadian Federation of Independent Business in 2004, an astounding 51 percent of respondents didn't sell abroad because their products or services were 'not exportable.' . . . [The] Toronto Dominion Bank quickly jumped on the finding, asking, 'In this day and age, what *isn't* a global product?' ")[1]

We hope that this book can be as useful to our neighbors to the north as it is to organizations in the United States. Indeed, given that the United States and Canada have the world's most active trading partnership, much of what we have to say may be useful to American companies exporting to Canada and vice versa. Both cultures share a great deal in common, including a proclivity to make the same mistakes in sending the wrong people abroad. We have a lot to learn from each other—and, more important here, a lot to learn about doing business with other parts of the world.

THE GOAL OF GETTING IT RIGHT

Are you responsible for choosing the people your organization sends overseas? These can be management staff, roving representatives, administrative support people, engineers, or anyone who will be representing *your* organization or company to another

---

1. Andrea Mandel-Campbell, *Why Mexicans Don't Drink Molson: Rescuing Canadian Business from the Suds of Global Obscurity* (Vancouver, BC: Douglas & McIntyre, 2007), 27, 35.

part of the world. Then you need this book. Are you looking for an overseas assignment yourself, to broaden your experience and boost your career? You need this book, too.

Whether you work for a large multinational company, a small enterprise launching into the international arena for the first time, a nongovernmental organization, or a university—you want to be *effective*. The late management guru Peter F. Drucker (a colleague of one of the authors) used to stress two things constantly. First, that the difference between *efficient* and *effective* is that being *efficient* means doing something right; whereas being *effective* means *doing the right thing*. This is a crucial difference many of us confuse. Second, he reminded us that no matter what our role is in an organization, the idea that should be overarching everything else in our minds is *contribution*. What should we be contributing to our organization?

When you send people overseas, you can't be effective unless you send the right people. If you go overseas, you need to be right for the assignment. It's as simple as that.

This is a book about international business. But it also applies to any noncommercial institution or organization that needs to send people overseas. Specifically, it's about one of the most basic tools of international business and relations—sending your employees overseas.

But this book will not be useful for every business that sends people overseas. If your organization uses overseas assignments as rewards or perks or punishments or for "diversity" or as part of a "career track" or for any reason other than to get tasks accomplished, this book isn't for you. (We'd like to change your mind and persuade you that such an approach can only result in failure; see if you agree with us by the end of this book!)

If, on the other hand, you view international expansion as a way to get something done—if you have identified something that will benefit your organization and you need to send the best person abroad to make that happen—then this book will help you.

We don't guarantee success—that hinges on far too many factors, and every good manager knows that there are no credible guarantees—but we can help with one crucial, usually overlooked first step: choosing whom to send.

The book you're holding in your hands will be your friendly guide on how to do it right. Filled with stories and anecdotes (some of them pretty shocking) from our many years in the international arena, *Carry a Chicken in Your Lap* will help you to send the right people, for the right reasons, to globalize your business.

A ROAD MAP TO WHERE WE'RE GOING

The book is organized into four main areas. First, in this introduction, plus the next chapter, we'll lay out the argument for why it's important to go overseas, and what the key considerations are. Next, we'll spend four chapters talking about what it takes to be successful overseas—and what characteristics lead expatriates to fail. We're making two central points here. First, *not everybody can do this.* Although Americans and Canadians are fond of imagining that any one of us can master anything if we just try hard enough, this is manifestly *not* the case in the international arena. Some people just can't overcome some of the hurdles we'll discuss— any one of which can render an assignment useless or even counterproductive and dangerous!

Second, the characteristics needed for success in the international arena—the things that you should be looking for in your people—aren't the things we usually look for, and they aren't usually found on a résumé. Which means you're going to have to do your homework by *getting to know your people well.* This is a theme we'll hit throughout the book—there's no substitute for knowing whom you're working with and what their strengths and weaknesses are. We don't offer foolproof international ability tests or ten-step checklists. There are no magic bullets here. What we *will* do is guide you in the kinds of honest conversations you need to be having with your employees.

Having given you a picture of what to look for in employees to send overseas, we'll spend a couple of chapters talking about *how,* and some of the obstacles that keep companies from doing this the right way. That will lead us into the third major area of the book: the *context* of sending people abroad. Here we'll talk not only about the mistakes companies make in their selection processes, but problems in dealing with corruption (it's not called the *Foreign Corrupt Practices Act* for nothing), international politics (yes, politics *does* matter in international business, far more than in your domestic market at home!), and with partners overseas (whom can you trust?). Some of these things affect whom you choose to send, and most of them affect *what you send them to do.* They are crucial parts of the picture, and we'd be remiss if we didn't offer you at least an introduction to them.

Finally, we'll turn the whole book on its head and talk about things from the other side: the perspective of someone who wants to be sent abroad. Much of this book is written for managers, executives, and human resources professionals who send people abroad to represent their company. But if you want to be the one who gets sent—if you're looking to internationalize your career— there's a lot here for you as well. We've got two chapters devoted to addressing two key questions: *should* you go overseas, and if so, how should you prepare and market yourself? If this describes you, read the rest of the book, too—there's a lot of useful stuff that you'll need to know!

Globalizing a business is exciting. Overseas markets at their best represent new business opportunities, as well as new opportunities to learn. They also involve enormous challenges. And in the present climate of economic uncertainty in the United States and Canada, they may hold the lifeline of survival for your company— if you can get it right and get the right people over there.

Let's get started!

2

Why Go Overseas?

AT THIS POINT, YOU may be saying to yourself, jeez, this sounds like a bunch of trouble. "Overseas" is a place where my employees may get dragged off planes and whipped, and where I could lose millions of dollars? No thanks. I'll stick with what I'm doing now, thank you very much.

Indeed, a great many American and Canadian companies have made exactly that argument. They vote with their feet by staying at home, plying their trade in the same well-worn paths in their regional domestic markets, hoping someday maybe to branch out all the way to the other end of the country. Chances are, if you've at least picked up this book, you aren't 100 percent committed to that strategy—you're at least *thinking* about taking your organization global, if not already in the midst of doing it. But you may have colleagues, managers, board members, or other stakeholders who do think this way. Chances are that *somebody* is going to feed you this argument at some point.

We have written this book on a fundamental premise: that going global is very likely in the near future to be a good thing for most businesses and many nonprofit organizations. We believe that current circumstances are going to make this strategy *necessary* for many, not just an option. Even in an economic downturn—in fact, because of it—getting your business or organization overseas is a fundamentally sound strategy. For the rest of this book to make sense, and to be useful, we need to explain why.

An important note on timing. We're writing this book at the beginning of 2009. Some of what we have to say here is connected to events and forces operating now, in the midst of a severe recession. We're not fortune-tellers, so we don't know exactly how things will look when you're reading this. But the outlines are pretty clear.

Note that much of what we have to say throughout the book is *not* dependent on this particular time or economic situation. Some of the trends discussed below have been a long time in the making and will not be reversed anytime soon—if ever. Some reasons for going global are as old as business itself and never change. We believe that now—that is, the time in which we are writing this book, and for the next few years—is a particularly auspicious moment to be thinking about globalizing your organization. But we also hope that you will find the book relevant whatever your present circumstances may be, because crossing borders and finding ways to partner with others around the world will always be important—and it will also be crucial that you have the right people to do the job.

WHEN YOU CAN'T PLAY IN YOUR OWN BACKYARD

Why is now a particularly good time to consider globalizing your organization? It's no secret that the U.S. and Canadian economies are in the throes of a serious recession. By the end of 2008, the

American economy had already experienced a year's worth of recession. More than 1.5 million jobs were lost in the United States in 2008. Personal income, industrial production, housing starts—a broad swath of economic indicators all dropped for most of the year, with 2009 promising to bring more of the same. The last two quarters of 2008 saw real GDP declines that accelerated through December, with no letup in sight. Canada's economy has not fared any better—it shed tens of thousands of jobs in 2008, reaching an unemployment rate near 6.5 percent and likely to go higher in 2009. The drop in commodity prices in late 2008 took a severe toll on the one sector of the Canadian economy doing reasonably well. All of these forces are expected to continue through 2009, with many of the effects being felt well into 2010. Of course, this is all as of this writing. By the time you pick up this book, things could be getting better—or they could be considerably worse.

What does this recession, or even depression, mean? For businesses, it means a serious drop-off in domestic markets. If you sell your product or service to Americans and Canadians, you're almost guaranteed to be selling less of it than you were two years ago—probably substantially less. Depending on what you sell, you may not see that market rebound for a very long time.

If this is you, the conclusion is obvious—*you need to find new markets*. Waiting for a market rebound at home isn't a strategy, it's a default mode. Although we're used to assuming that if the United States is in a recession, everywhere else is worse, this isn't true anymore. Chances are good that parts of the world are recovering fast. Some have undoubtedly weathered the storm better than North America. We'll talk more about the shifting role the United States plays in the world later in the book—for now, understand that just because the American economy has led the world into a downturn doesn't mean it will lead the way out again.

Peter Drucker was fond of reminding us that "the purpose of a business is to create a customer." When your existing pool of customers has dried up, you've got to go look for them somewhere else. If what you produce has value, then somewhere in the world someone is bound to want it and be willing to pay for it. At a time when American and Canadian customers aren't buying, why *wouldn't* you want to go look for new ones elsewhere?

NOT YOUR PARENTS' DOLLAR ANYMORE

One of the effects of the global economic shake-up has been to change the position of the U.S. dollar in the world's currency system. Because of the rules worked out in the Bretton Woods system at the end of World War II, the U.S. dollar has had a privileged place in the world economy, as the "world's reserve currency." This has given the U.S. dollar all sorts of advantages—as a safe haven for investors, as an international medium of exchange, as the dominant currency in oil, etc. Certain countries in Latin America have even adopted the U.S. dollar as legal currency there. And foreign governments have tended to keep large stocks of dollars in their reserve funds and central banks.

This has been good for American companies who get paid in U.S. dollars, but it has also tended to put up a barrier to exporting, especially when the American currency is strong—which tends to make American goods and services expensive. It has also had some advantages for Canadian companies, since the Canadian and U.S. dollars are easily convertible. It has also made it easier for Canadians to export into the United States, since the Canadian dollar historically tends to run weaker than its cousin to the south, making Canadian products relatively cheaper. With the American market now declining, of course, this last advantage doesn't mean much anymore. In fact, this has meant a lot of pain for Canadian companies, since in recent years more than three-quarters of Canada's exports have gone to the United States.

The U.S. dollar has been in a long-term slide for some time now, though it took the onset of a major recession for people to really start noticing and to accelerate the process. When the euro was first introduced as a European currency in 1999, it was valued at about €0.85 per US$1. This quickly rose to €1.1 per $1 in 2002, leading many at the time to assume that the euro would be a perpetually weak currency against the dollar. Six years later, one U.S. dollar will get you only €0.71—a devaluation of over 36 percent—and the dollar's value is falling still. Similar stories could be told of most of the world's other major currencies—the U.S. dollar lost over 35 percent against the Japanese yen, 28 percent against the British pound, and 30 percent against the Canadian dollar over the same period.

Some of the forces behind this decline have been building for some time, while others are quite recent. Despite public trust, most politicians are woefully uninformed about economics. They do not understand the long-term consequences of certain policy decisions. When Bruce was a senior fellow at a major American think tank, he spent considerable time on this point alone, working with (at the time) British prime minister Tony Blair's economic adviser to try to elevate public understanding. One of the most egregiously misunderstood laws of economics is that when a government prints more money than there are goods and services in the economy to "chase" those dollars, or absorb them, inflation *has* to be the result—a weakened dollar in terms of purchasing power and in terms of foreign currency exchanges, or forex. (Rising prices are not inflation; they are the *effect* of inflation.) At the time of this writing, few Americans and Canadians realize that the U.S. government is printing money at the rate of $11 *billion* per day.

The consequences of this are that slowly—perhaps over six months to a year—foreign investors will lose their confidence in the U.S. dollar and will begin to abandon their investments in U.S. Treasury instruments (bonds, T-bills, etc.). But this actually works in favor of American companies, for this means that the value of the U.S. dollar will keep dropping—meaning that your goods and services will be more affordable to those overseas (that is, they can buy more affordably, because they need fewer units of their own currency to pay against your invoices in U.S. dollars).

Put somewhat differently, the blizzard of U.S. government spending and lending—$700 billion for the TARP financial bailout, an additional $2 trillion (and rising) in Federal Reserve lending, billions more for bailouts of this and that industry, not to mention the ongoing U.S. government deficit—has created a massive influx of U.S. dollars into the world economy. You don't need a math degree from Caltech to know what happens anytime you quickly flood a market with massive amounts of something: the price or value of that something—including currency—goes down. Way down.

How is all of this related to the need to take your business global? American and Canadian firms are facing a new world, one in which the U.S. dollar is no longer king. For example, most professional currency traders acknowledge that China has launched a well-organized campaign to replace the U.S. dollar as the world's major trade currency. If previously companies in other countries sought to be paid in U.S. dollars for their safety and strength, today the opposite is true—North American firms need sources of other currency to get around the weakness of the dollar. We can't predict what the precise exchange rates will be when you read this, but ask yourself: would I prefer today that my company be paid in U.S. dollars, or in euros, Swiss francs, or Japanese yen?

Remember the upside to all of this. With the U.S. dollar down (and given the closeness of their economies, the Canadian dollar likely down with it), your goods and services are becoming *much more affordable* in other parts of the world. A dollar dive and high inflation in North America are *the* best reasons to go find those parts of the world that are *not* in inflationary spirals. This is where the customers are who can afford, and will buy, your products and services. This is also where you can find new partners to strengthen your business at home—the last weak-dollar, high-inflation period in the 1980s resulted in an enormous influx of new investment into the United States and Canada.

This is true even in parts of the world that don't have ready access to "hard currency"—that is, major currencies that are easily convertible into U.S. or Canadian dollars. Let's face yet another harsh truth: this recession is going to impact all regions in the world, not just North America. Although your goods and services are definitely going to be more affordable with a weaker dollar, some countries are going to lack the hard-currency reserves they need to buy your products. Must you then just walk away? Be assured that most companies will. But why not take a more informed, contrarian approach and service the markets that most are going to ignore? Instead of thinking in the conventional way—insisting on confirmed letters of credit drawn in U.S. dollars, for example—why not consider using more advanced techniques such as countertrade? Countertrade is not barter. It's much more powerful and is used when a country does not have goods and services you'd be willing to trade in lieu of cash dollars. It is a financial technique that often lets you sell without any competition at all and be paid in U.S. or Canadian dollars (or another chosen hard currency).

You should never attempt a countertrade transaction on your own. But specialists out there—including our company—know how to structure them for you and ensure your payment through a skillfully devised protocol document that links all the elements of a countertrade transaction together. To give you one example, Bruce structured a successful countertrade program for a British industrial client a few years back. The client was the regular provider of sugar-refining equipment to the government of Cuba. Sugar being Cuba's principal export (and thus the principal hard-currency earner for the country), the government was desperate to keep the refining going. Unfortunately, sugar prices had dramatically dropped, which reduced income to Havana. Cuba suddenly found itself unable to pay for spare parts for the refining equipment it already had. (Remember that countries with weak currencies depend on being paid in hard currencies for their exports.)

The British company retained Bruce to devise a countertrade

program that would enable them to be paid in some hard currency, so that they could in fact extend spares coverage to the Cubans and even possibly sell them more needed equipment. It presented a special challenge because Cuba had for nearly half a century been isolated economically through various embargoes, and it stood politically at a distance from many other countries. This limited their options. Although it took a few months, Bruce used his Hollywood contacts to identify a major production company that wanted to film a major movie in Havana. After obtaining a forecast budget, he approached the Cuban government. Bruce explained that the production of the film would entail huge expenses in local currency (Cuban pesos): salaries, pay for walkons and extras, food, accommodation, technical crews, equipment, and much more. Since all of these expenses would have to be paid in local Cuban currency, would Havana be willing to pay these expenses for the film company, in exchange for being released from their obligations to the British company? Once Bruce had that agreement in place, a protocol agreement was drafted that linked this step to the next one: the Hollywood producer agreed to pay $20 million to the British equipment supplier, and the Cuban government agreed to pay the equivalent of US$20 million in local expenses inside Cuba. All parties won: the British were paid, the Cubans got their spare parts, and the movie was produced. This is the power of countertrade executed properly. It can open many markets to you that would otherwise remain closed.

NOT JUST NOW, BUT INTO THE FUTURE

What we've given you so far are reasons why you should consider globalizing your business *now*. But you might argue, "Well, we'll just wait this out, and things will go back to normal—then we can get back to doing business at home the way we've always done."

This might actually work in some corners of the economy. But we can't name them easily, and the chances that you are in one are small. Writ broadly, what we're seeing is not simply a dip in the road or a downturn in the regular business cycle. In the back of this book, you'll see a collection of readings we recommend that go into much greater detail about the sea changes we're referring to here. But the bottom line is simple: things aren't going back to "normal," at least not if you define "normal" as the United States and Canada being able to look in at themselves and ignore the world outside North America.

This isn't a particularly new insight—globalization arguments have been around at least since the 1970s. Since that time, a lot of sectors of the U.S. and Canadian economies *have* reached out to other parts of the world. But a lot haven't. "Global" became associated with "large," so that while some small and medium-size companies have ventured abroad, many thought they couldn't. With periods of sustained growth in the American and Canadian economies in the 1980s, 1990s, and 2000s, it has simply been easier to work the domestic markets, maybe dabble a little in Europe, and leave the rest of the world alone.

Clearly, we no longer have that luxury. Moreover, our argument here is that *it isn't coming back*. We'll talk more later in the book about the position the United States has held in the world, what this position has meant for American businesses overseas, and how it's changing. For now, we simply want to make the point that this is *not* a flash-in-the-pan exercise. We're entering a period in which global business is not a luxury. It's not a strategy for growth. It's a necessity for survival.

The recession and financial crisis that slammed into America in 2008 made its debut on Wall Street. Up until then, a popular mantra in America and Canada was that debt was the handmaiden of growth. But we know better now. Debt is a *cost*, and it must always be viewed that way. Countless decent businesses have been completely wiped out by debt: their cash flow was strong, but their debt-service costs (interest and principal payments) were so high that the companies could not survive. Sadly, the cost of debt is also sweeping through the international arena, corporate and government alike. This makes predictability very difficult, but this is a certainty: if you keep your organization's leverage (the ratio of debt to equity) low, you will likely survive the recession and be able to hire the people you need to optimize your performance around the world.

WHAT IF MY ORGANIZATION DOESN'T WANT TO MAKE MONEY?

These arguments have so far all been aimed at *businesses*— organizations that exist to make a profit by selling some product or service to customers. The logic for businesses to go global is pretty pressing: the customers at home have stopped buying, people in other parts of the world can buy American and Canadian goods and services cheaply, so that's where the customers are. But what if your organization isn't a business? We hope that this book will be useful to you as well—all kinds of organizations can benefit from taking their operations global. To do that, you need the right people in place.

But why is going global important if you're not trying to make money? Nonprofit organizations have much to gain from globalizing their operations, or reaching out to find partners overseas. Consider funding sources. In the current economic climate, how well are your domestic funding sources doing? Many nonprofit foundations that relied on invested endowments have been seriously damaged or wiped out by the crash on Wall Street. One lesson to draw from that experience is that U.S. markets aren't the safest place to keep all your money. But where else would you put it, and with whom? That involves finding the right global partners and working with them.

Maybe your funding comes from donors. If so, chances are

good that donations have been down in the past year or two—perhaps precipitously so. Who else has money and might be interested in your cause? Americans and Canadians are used to thinking of philanthropy as something that flows outward—we send our money to other parts of the world, however they don't send it here. But the world is changing, and this is likely to change, too. You will need to find new global partners and learn to work with them.

Finally, nonprofit organizations, whatever their mission, are similar to businesses in that they run on *innovation* and *ideas*. Who's to say the best innovations and the most effective ideas are found at home? Whatever issue your organization addresses, chances are that dozens of other organizations around the planet are working on the same issue. Think you might have something to learn from them? You probably do—if you can find the right partnerships and work together.

WHAT ABOUT ME? SHOULD MY CAREER GO GLOBAL?

Everything we've written above applies to *organizations*. We think that nearly every organization has something to gain by pursuing global connections, and that for many it is becoming a matter of survival. So the arguments we've laid out in this chapter speak to the people who run those organizations, set their strategies, and make the decisions on whether to go global.

But maybe you don't run the organization. Maybe you just work in it. Perhaps you work in an organization that is already globalized, and you're wondering whether you should join that path and make your own career international. Or perhaps you're in a company that is considering expanding abroad, and you might be in a position to jump in early. Are there reasons for you to think about globalizing *your* career?

First, a preview. We have two chapters, near the end of this book, dedicated entirely to you. We think you should read the rest of the book first, but in those chapters you'll find a lot of advice on answering two key questions: Am *I* the right person to go overseas? And if so, how do I set myself up to do that? If you are already thinking about taking your career international, those chapters are for you.

But what about that first part? What motivation is there for you, an individual worker, to consider internationalizing your career path? It's easy for a CEO or a manager at the top to make that decision for the organization—chances are, other people are going to have to carry it out. But deciding you want to take your career overseas yourself means *you* are the one to go. You have to uproot your life, pack, move to a strange land, far from the center of corporate power and watercooler gossip, with a strange language and strange customs. Why would you want to do that?

For some, the answer lies in their own experience. Many Americans and Canadians who go overseas early in life—studying abroad in college, for example, or traveling with family—get bitten by the "international bug." They fall in love with a foreign land. They learn the language and enjoy the contrast of cultures. They thrive on new experiences—new food, new music, new rhythms of life. If this is you, we don't have to sell you on the idea of working overseas; we just have to show you what it takes to do it successfully.

But this may not be you. Maybe you haven't traveled much outside North America. Maybe you're not sure what it would be like living and working in a foreign culture. How well would you do? Could you do it successfully? If these are your questions, this is the right book to read. In the following chapters, we will show you what it takes to succeed in the international arena, and you can decide for yourself whether you have what it takes. One of our lessons throughout the book is, if you're not right for the job, don't try it!

But there are good reasons to figure out whether this is for you or not, even if you don't already have a yearning to work overseas. Many of these reasons relate to the economic picture we spelled out above. Whatever the details of today's stock market or financial indexes, the broader realities are clear. The productive forces of the world economy—the places where real wealth is generated, and where the opportunities can be found—are increasingly spread around the globe, and less and less concentrated in the United States and Canada.

Over time, this will mean that parts of the world that are becoming more productive and wealthy will become nicer places to live. Some of them (Switzerland and Sweden, for example, in our opinion) already *are* nicer places to live—and have been for some time. Job opportunities, purchasing power, low crime, quality of life—all of these will increasingly be found on other shores. That's not to say that the United States and Canada are going to become unlivable Third World countries. But they will not have the dominance of opportunities they once did. Whatever you want in life, chances are good that, starting today, there will be more and more opportunities to find it abroad. So *do* take the time to read through this book. Consider whether you have what it takes to succeed internationally. If you do, you will discover—literally—a whole new world of possibilities open to you.

SUMMARY

We're writing this book at the beginning of 2009, looking out toward the next couple of years. We don't have a crystal ball that tells exactly what will happen when, but the broad outlines are pretty clear. The world is changing in ways that make it increasingly imperative for your organization—whatever its mission or market niche—to globalize its operations. The forces pushing all of this may be complicated, but the effects are simple and easy to see:

- The U.S. and Canadian domestic markets have been shrinking significantly. A domestic-market-only strategy is no longer a viable option.
- The U.S. dollar has substantially slid in value and is losing its status as the world's reserve currency. This is making American and Canadian goods and services increasingly price-competitive around the world.
- The changes of the past year or two are the culmination of much larger structural changes that have substantially shifted the balance of economic and productive power. Future strategy needs to reflect these realities.
- Nonprofit organizations are not immune to these forces. They, too, need to globalize—to find new places to invest endowment funds, to locate new donors, and to develop partnerships to generate new ideas and new approaches.
- Individuals need to think about globalizing their careers for many of the same reasons—fewer opportunities at home, more overseas.

What we've laid out here is an argument for *why* you need to globalize. Hopefully you agree—indeed, you may already have come to this conclusion. This sets up the key question for this book: *how*. Our argument is simple: *you need to send the right people*. How do you do that? Read on . . .

3

I'm Not a Racist!

THE HEAD OF INTERNATIONAL marketing for a Fortune 1000 company was new to the job. He told Bruce he needed no outside assistance in helping his company break into new markets. When asked how he was going to tackle the East European market for his product line, you can only imagine Bruce's astonishment when he replied that he was sending a young Polish woman from Warsaw to Moscow "to tap the Russian market" and would then export from Russia into East Europe!

That strategy has so many dreadful mistakes that it boggles the mind of a seasoned internationalist. First, the resentment between Poland and Russia is as old as the history of Europe, and darkly serious. Although trade definitely flows through both countries, tensions are real and historically grounded. To send a woman *from Poland* into Moscow would not be at all well received by Russian executives—even though North Americans would understandably resent being told that (a conundrum addressed fully in this chapter). But to send a *young* woman was even more offensive to the Russian hosts.

We in North America often tend to think of race in terms of color, but this is wrong. Russians are as separate a race from Poles as Ugandans are from South Africans (though the same outer color). In this case, the company proposed to compound this error with another faux pas: by selling American-brand products into East Europe from Russia. This is not a race issue, it is cultural. Having been under the tyranny of the hammer and sickle of Soviet communism for half a century, East Europeans are only now shedding the deep resentment they feel for any consumer goods originating in Russia. This company's strategy was doomed to failure because of the inability to take seriously issues of race and gender in the international arena. We've got to tackle them here.

We are making one assumption in writing this chapter—and in placing it right up front in the book. That assumption is that you want the best for your organization. You want it to thrive, you want your people to thrive, and you want to maximize your chances of success. That does *not* mean that you don't also value other things—such as fairness and equity and treating your people with respect. Indeed, part of what we're going to argue here is that you show respect for your people when you put them in a position to succeed.

We state this up front because of all the writing about issues of gender, race, and religion—but especially gender. A lot of this writing stems from the excellent instincts of American and Canadian society to be fair and to treat people equally before the law. These are certainly understandable: we all agree that discrimination in the workplace for things that don't have anything to do with job performance is unjust. You can't put all your red-haired people in lousy jobs just because you don't like people with red hair.

However, plenty of perfectly legal and warranted discrimination occurs in workplaces, on issues where characteristics *are* related to job performance. With due apologies to Spud Webb, very few guys under five feet seven inches play in the NBA. On the other hand, men and women over six feet three inches don't generally get hired as flight attendants. And men who weigh one hundred pounds don't often get to play professional hockey. Why? Because these things affect how well people can do those jobs.

So we want to put our premise up front here, as we have in the chapter title. We're not racists, or sexists, or –ists of any sort. We believe in the equality of individuals before the law, and in treating people fairly on the basis of their merits.

The harsh truth, though, is that people outside North America generally see things a lot differently than we do. It's all well and good to talk about the value of global diversity—and a lot of that diversity *is* valuable. But sometimes diversity means that other cultures have very different ways of looking at the world—ways that may disagree with ours. That's reality. In a couple of chapters we'll write about how trying to change that reality can get you into serious trouble. For now, please accept the premise that our primary goal here is the same as yours: to maximize the chances of success in your business in the face of international realities.

GENDER GAPS AND DOUBLE STANDARDS: WOMEN IN INTERNATIONAL BUSINESS

A lot of the writing on gender and overseas postings stems from a basic observation: although women have done well in climbing the corporate ladder to managerial positions here in North America, most people sent abroad by companies are men. Surveys indicate that women account for around only 15 percent of overseas assignments by American companies, for a number of reasons. However, much of the writing on the subject is designed to tease out how much of this is due to gender discrimination.

That's unfortunate, because although gender discrimination does undoubtedly (and wrongly) play a role in some cases, other factors are at work—some of which can impact whether your people are successful in their international assignments. Interestingly, some surveys suggest that women often take *themselves* out of the running for international work, especially if it involves going to a country that is very culturally different from North America or less developed—and often, of course, those go together.[1]

So does it matter whether you're a man or a woman when you go to do business abroad? Yes—sometimes. Certainly, in many Western (or westernized) countries gender doesn't matter much, if at all. But in other places gender may cause cultural clashes.

Sometimes the clues are fairly evident. In some East Asian countries, for example, it is easy to observe gender imbalances in the workplace, where the majority of lower-level workers may be women but almost all of the managers are men. In at least one case of an Asian company, these attitudes had even been passed to its foreign subsidiary in North America. The subsidiary had hired a recruitment firm to help bring in prospective employees. Even though the HR manager of the subsidiary was North American, he echoed the culture of the parent company and its homeland: he ordered the recruitment firm to "stop sending résumés of women and blacks," saying he would "hire as few as possible." The recruiter refused to comply and the contract was terminated, leading to a lawsuit—and a messy example of how culture, gender, and race can sometimes collide like a train crash.

Another study in a pair of similar East Asian countries found a similar result. Executives were given the task of choosing a manager for the local subsidiary of a hypothetical American company. Four candidates were offered, the most obviously qualified

---

1. Kevin Lowe, Meredith Downes, and K. Galen Kroeck, "The Impact of Gender and Location on the Willingness to Accept Overseas Assignments," *International Journal of Human Resource Management* 10, no. 2 (April 1999): 223–34.

of whom was a black woman. In at least one sample, less than 10 percent of the local executives chose this candidate, and she ended up dead last in their overall preferences. Even when the experiment was changed so the top performer was a white woman, the choices were similar. Interestingly, when executives were asked to choose the head of a multinational from their home country operating in the United States, the effect disappeared—they seemed perfectly happy to have a black woman working for them, just not in their own country.[2] Like it or not, discrimination *does* exist, and other countries may not have the same legal frameworks to deal with it.

Gender and race can combine in different ways. Many Western businesses operate on Taiwan, which has an interesting mix of a Western-oriented economy and a Chinese cultural heritage. In that setting, white women from America report being treated more like foreigners than like women—that is, they are expected to be different and are treated differently because they're not Chinese. But Chinese-American women sent into the same environment can be subjected to a lot more gender discrimination and harassment—they are expected to meet the local standards for "female" behavior and don't "count" as foreigners.

Sometimes you don't get the benefits of a double standard—cultural rules are rules. We began this book with a dramatic story of a woman flying into a Middle Eastern country and being summarily deported. But companies make that mistake all the time. Some years ago, a Spanish company sent a delegation to the Middle East that included a number of women dressed in the height of European style—a not uncommon strategy in sales. These women fared no better than the woman on Bruce's plane did—they were

---

2. Rosalie Tung, "Do Race and Gender Matter in International Assignments to/from Asia Pacific?" *Human Resource Management* 47, no. 1 (Spring 2008): 91–110.

immediately shipped out of the country on the next flight, and the company lost the sale.

All of this is *not* to make the argument that women should not be sent on international assignments. But for *some* assignments, a woman is likely not the best choice. Women who are sent overseas *must* be able to adjust to cultural expectations about gender that are *radically* different from those in the United States and Canada. Most of us in the workplace today have lived with a generation or more of the truth that women are just as qualified as men, and we've seen a lot of formerly male-dominated jobs (doctor, lawyer, manager) welcome women into their ranks. But some other parts of the world haven't followed us in this, and many won't for a long time, if ever. If you want your people to succeed on international assignments, you have to make sure they can check their gender expectations at the door and know what they are and aren't willing to do to adapt.

COLOR-BLIND? RACE AND OVERSEAS ASSIGNMENTS

Race can play a similar role in many situations. Think back to the true story that opened this chapter. A lot of the time, it is simple common sense. For example, is it prudent to send North American Jews into Arab countries? Simple answer: no. A few Middle East countries will usually accept them as assigned expatriates (especially if they have some special talent that is badly needed in the country), but their lives will be torturous. We know because Bruce has lived in the Middle East and worked with Jews who have valiantly tried to make effective contributions, only to be reduced to tears. Too, it is most unfair for their families—if their families are even given visas. We all hope this will change over time, but, again, simple history—in this case several thousand years of it—suggests that a resolution will not soon be effected.

"Race" or ethnic background can even play a role in cases

where outsiders can't tell the difference. Sometimes categories are different in other parts of the world. Some years ago, Bill met a young African-American academic who had grown up in the United States and had spent some time studying African politics in African countries. In an interview, he recounted how, for the first time in his life, people treated him as white—not just in subtle ways, but even in speaking to him. When he tried to protest to the locals that he was just like them, they said, "No, you are American, you are white." In that part of the world, "white" meant not the color of his skin but what clothes he wore and how he talked—which were, of course, indistinguishable from any other well-educated (white) American.

Even within countries, background distinctions can matter a lot. A major electronics company sent a team to a plant in Sicily that was having difficulties. The team had been carefully chosen to include a number of Italian-Americans who spoke fluent Italian, to make communication with the local management and workers easy. But when they got there, they had trouble getting any meaningful cooperation from the locals—not because of language difficulties but because the team members' families had all come from mainland Italy, not from Sicily! Local Sicilians distrusted "mainlanders" and considered them a separate group, instead of being part of the "Italian nation."

Issues of racism can cut both ways. Not only is it ill-advised to send someone from your company who is likely to meet resistance and discrimination, but you should also be careful to avoid sending your own employees if *they* are racists! A U.S. bank was once negotiating with a major oil-producing Arab country over the sale of materials for cleaning up oil spills. The final negotiations took place in Switzerland, a classically neutral location. The senior American banker had brought an assistant with him to help with the finer details of financing the deal. But when the assistant was asked how he wanted the financing handled, he replied, "It doesn't matter unless the buyers are Arabs. You can't trust those Arabs."

The senior banker was able to save the deal through profuse apologies, but only on condition that the assistant be removed from the negotiations entirely.[3]

Racism can come from all corners. Turkey is a complex, fascinating country that rightly prides itself as being a bridge between East and West. When it became a republic in the early 1920s under the enlightened rule of Mustafa Kemal Atatürk (who gave women the vote and the right to divorce and to own land, and simplified the language), the country found itself suddenly catapulted into entirely new relations with Europe—almost overnight. Assigned to live in Turkey for a year and a half in 1969, Bruce was on a train from Istanbul to Ankara, reading about that tumultuous period. Suddenly the distinguished, elderly gentleman sitting next to him said in a surprisingly gentle voice, "You know, there's really more to that story than you know." The man was Selçuk Gemüşpala (which means "silver sword"), who was formerly the right hand of Atatürk.

Invited to join Selçuk-bey as his guest for dinner in the dining car, Bruce listened with rapt attention as the senior statesman related the story of a grand meeting with top British officials in London in 1926. "As you can imagine, Atatürk was a commanding presence. Everyone in that room knew that he had literally ended the five-hundred-year reign of the Ottoman Empire and had given birth to a republic that he wanted badly to be accepted by the West. Although he spoke little English, he understood it surprisingly well—a fact not known by our hosts in London. The discussion on the table concerned the Dardanelles, that stretch of water that connects the Black Sea and the Mediterranean, and the Turkish land on either side of it. Frustrated by Turkey's reluctance to cede any of its territory to others, one member of the House of

---

3. David Ricks, *Blunders in International Business* (Oxford: Blackwell, 1999), 100–101.

Lords muttered, 'Well, what can we expect from a Turkish barbarian?' I flinched. I looked over at Atatürk, seated next to me. He was staring placidly straight ahead, unmoved. But his right hand was moving furiously with his pen. 'Say this, please!' he whispered in my ear as he pushed the note over to me. I cleared my throat and translated quickly into English, 'Your Lordship, even Turkish barbarians respect the notion of national sovereignty as set out in the Treaty of Westphalia in 1648. And while we acknowledge that it was not signed formally by England, it was nevertheless respected by King Charles the First and by every British regent thereafter.' The silence in that room I shall never forget!'"

Make sure, when you are choosing your people to send overseas, that you don't export the wrong attitudes. This may require some careful investigation—a subject we'll talk more about in chapter 7.

GOD IN THE FACTORY: RELIGION AND BUSINESS

Local feelings about religion can be just as important as attitudes toward gender and race. The basic rule is the same—understand that other people see the world very differently, and make sure the people you send overseas are prepared to respect that.

Often the problem is not the religion per se, but the boundaries that religion places on behavior. In the United States and Canada we are used to being able to freely choose our religious practices, and to being protected from having others impose their religious beliefs on us. If people want to wear crosses or dress in plain, homemade clothing or wear turbans, that's fine. Even in the aftermath of 9/11 and the "war on terror," North America has seen no major battles over Muslim headscarves, as some European countries have. So we're used to drawing a line between the private religious arena and tolerance for different choices in public.

That line doesn't exist in some other parts of the world, and you have to make sure that the people you send overseas understand that and can adapt to it. The international business community saw a dramatic example in the summer of 2008. Two British citizens, a man and a woman, were caught being intimate on a beach in Dubai—a crime according to that country's Islamic laws. They had been drinking—another potential crime, though the law is not generally enforced on foreigners—and had gotten carried away with themselves. For crossing this line, the two were jailed and put on trial. The man had come to Dubai to set up a business, a plan he had to abandon. After three months, both were deported from the country—ending two international business careers in Dubai with a single careless act.

Like gender expectations, religion can be carried by the people you send and can get in the way of their effectiveness. There is an old African saying: "God save us from missionaries!" We will write more in a couple of chapters about the importance of not sending people who want to change the world. But religion is a particular category here—at once a personal trait and, sometimes, a motivator that can get expatriates in trouble.

Bruce resided in a country in Africa known for its wide religious tolerance. Jews, Muslims, Christians, and atheists lived among one another without incident. But one day a large North American corporation sent a senior executive to reside there as the general manager of their regional operations. Managerially speaking, he was qualified. But he brought with him a zealous sense of religious superiority that, typically, manifested itself as rigid intolerance.

In his first week on the job, he screamed at Muslims who were in a corner observing one of the five prayer times of the day, and then at Sikhs whose heads were traditionally wrapped. By the next week, more than a hundred employees—excellent performers—had walked off the job. Some of them brought in government authorities to the site. The meeting between this executive and those government officials was acrimonious. In that meeting, the executive said that he would accept crosses as jewelry and pins, but no other expression of religious faith or identity! Even though the officials tried to explain the supreme importance of religious diversity and coexistence in their country, the response was an arrogant assertion of "rights" that the executive claimed he had—as a guest in a foreign country, no less.

Of course he had no such rights, and a week later the government informed the American corporate headquarters that this executive would have to be removed at once, or all government contracts with that company would be canceled and official hearings would be held for the aggrieved workers. This bitter experience could entirely have been avoided if the American firm had been aware of the importance of thoroughly screening its candidates for overseas postings with more understanding of what was important to the country of assignment.

If you can learn to check these instincts at the door, things usually go much more smoothly. Westerners are often surprised at how tolerant other religious traditions are. Greg Mortenson, the mountain-climber-turned-humanitarian who wrote the bestselling *Three Cups of Tea*, has spent years working in the mountains of Pakistan, one of the most conservative areas of the Islamic world. He is not a Muslim himself and has never made any attempt to convert to Islam. But his respect for local ways has earned him widespread acceptance among people that many Americans assume would reject him out of hand.

The point here is not that employees with particular religious identities should or shouldn't be sent overseas. But whatever their own views, they *must* be able to take seriously the religious sensibilities of other cultures—even when those beliefs lead to very different rules (such as not being able to drink alcohol, or having to wear certain kinds of clothing). As with gender issues, they have to be able to leave their own religious expectations at home—not for themselves, but for the locals they'll be working with.

IF MOMMA AIN'T HAPPY: FAMILIES ABROAD

An old folk saying in the South of the United States goes "If Momma ain't happy, ain't nobody happy." There's a lot of wisdom in that, because a great many international-assignment failures are due not to problems with the person you sent, but with the family.

Occasionally, the spouse brings his or her own baggage along—everything written above applies to him or her as well. Husbands and wives often appear at social/business functions overseas with their spouse, and a spouse who can't adapt to local attitudes about gender roles, or who brings racist attitudes, or who wants to proselytize the locals, will land your company in just as much trouble as if your employee had done the same.

Another major American company sent a very competent executive to manage its South African operations when Bruce was living there. The executive behaved with a professionalism and decorum that set an inspiring example for others. But his wife was his opposite. She brought with her a rigid American belief that "the American way" (whatever that is!) is the *only* way. Within a few months she had thoroughly agitated local South African blacks and whites alike with her brash assertions about the purported superiority of everything American. The situation became so grave that the company had to send a senior level representative to make a special trip to South Africa to address the issue. Only when she was warned that the company would have no choice but to recall her husband (seriously harming his career and future) did she agree to desist. But the damage had been done, and even years later she is openly discussed as a "cultural terrorist" by locals who had experienced her inappropriate judgments.

A lot of problems come not from spouses who actively cause trouble, but from those who simply can't make the adjustment. This extends to the whole family—if the relocation involves children, their adjustment issues can cause problems for your employee as well—but it's particularly a problem for a trailing spouse. The employee has the work to focus on and is quickly forced to meet and interact with a range of new people, developing a social as well as a professional network. Children are often in school and find new friends and activities there that, if they adapt well, can be sustaining. But if the relocated spouse doesn't have a job—and often on long expatriate assignments she may not—that person doesn't have any built-in social network. Many times, spouses end up clustering together, much the way international students do on American and Canadian college campuses—there, but not quite a part of the crowd around them.

Posted to Sofia, Bulgaria, with her husband, one wife found herself not only lonely but intimidated by the strange language, the baffling Cyrillic alphabet, and the paucity of English. (This was only months after the fall of the Berlin Wall and the withdrawal of the Soviet Union from Eastern Europe.) Bruce suggested that she run an ad *in English* in one of the local newspapers, which she did. She sought new friends who spoke some English and would want an American friend in their circle. She was besieged with responses—eager notes to her PO box from Bulgarians who within weeks had warmed her life. Indeed, that one event may have enabled her to adjust so swiftly that the couple sought serial renewals of their posting to Bulgaria.

In another international posting, a spouse of an American executive wound up essentially alone all day in a house in a Paris suburb where hardly anyone spoke English. After a few weeks of pointing at the Camembert in the cheese shop, she enrolled in the Alliance Française and joined the local choral group, figuring rightly that music is a universal language. Helped by her new French singing friends, she became so fluent that she not only earned a teaching certificate (allowing her to teach French outside France) but also acted as an unpaid interpreter for the bewildered mothers in the next beds when she gave birth to her children at the misleadingly named American Hospital, where few of the doctors and fewer of the nurses spoke English. She later followed her husband to Hong Kong, where she joined the English Speaking Union, tutored Cantonese speakers, and was invited to lunch with the region's chief executive.

A philosopher of the twentieth century wrote, "The success is in the boldness!" No matter what country you are sent to, reach out to the local people with humility. You will be wonderfully surprised!

Children's adjustments can cause problems as well. Many of the seasoned managers that companies want to send overseas are in their late thirties or mid-forties and may have young or teenage children to move and educate as well. One American manager was offered opportunities in several different locations around the world, including Europe, China, and the Middle East. But his sixteen-year-old daughter didn't want to go to any of those places. She had friends and activities and connections to sports teams and bands—the kinds of things that teens do. She begged to be allowed to live with the neighbors rather than have to go abroad. Eventually, the manager had to turn down the international opportunities and remained in the United States, knowing that taking a reluctant daughter abroad would likely ruin his effectiveness on the job.

We'd like to offer a closing thought on the gender issue. We explained above that there *are,* whether we like it or not, places in this world to which North American companies and institutions would simply be foolish to send women. But in *many* places on this planet, women can perform brilliantly and effectively, and they should be given both the opportunities and encouragement by right-thinking employers. All of Europe, Australia, New Zealand, parts of Asia, quite a few parts of Latin America—these areas will almost always welcome prepared women who want only to be given the same work and opportunities of their male counterparts. The organization that is mindful of this will benefit its own bottom line as well as the lives of its women staff.

SUMMARY

In this chapter we've tried to take on some of the trickier—but also most important—issues involved with sending people overseas to represent your organization. Gender, race, religion, and family issues are often minefields where it's difficult to have honest and open conversations (we'll talk more about this in chapter 7 and again in chapter 14). But hopefully you've been impressed with the seriousness of the issues raised here:

- Take seriously the gender-role standards and expectations of the country to which you're sending your people.
- Stay true to your company's values of fairness and equity, but don't try to impose them on the rest of the world.
- Understand your employee's attitudes about gender roles, race, and religion; don't send somebody whose ideas and attitudes are going to clash with those of the locals (more on this in chapter 5).
- Know the relevant dimensions of race and division in the host country (e.g., don't send Poles to Russia, or Koreans to Japan). It's not always skin color; do your homework so you know what differences *do* matter.
- Know what your employee's family situation is, and whether sending this person on this assignment will cause problems for the family. Your most productive workers can be undermined by family problems.

A common thread runs through all of these: *know your employees!* We'll talk about this more in chapter 7. Dealing with the issues we've outlined here involves knowing who your employees are, and how well they will fit in the country to which you're considering sending them.

4

It's Not Just What You Say— It's How You Say It

BRUCE HAS SPENT MOST of his life working in the international arena. On a trip to Turkey with a client some years back, he warned the client to be exceptionally courteous in restaurants. One night, the client awakened him frantically, pounding on his hotel room door. Outside the door with him was a shouting man—a nearby restaurant manager—and a uniformed policeman who was none too amused. The client had insisted on eating out on his own that night. In the restaurant, unable to read a single word of Turkish, he had somehow managed to order a main course. Later he assumed the waiter was asking him about dessert. Having heard great things about the quality of Turkish peaches, he kept repeating, "Peach!" Over and over the client said this—even shouted it—oblivious to how all conversation abruptly stopped around him in the restaurant. Did the Turks hear the word *peach*? Oh, definitely. They heard, *"Piç!"*—pronounced exactly like *peach*, but meaning *bastard*! (The Turkish word for *peach* is *şeftalı*, pronounced *shef-TAH-luh*.) Not only are such words rarely used in Turkish culture, but the client's constant repetition and growing frustration upset the staff and nearby diners.

Bruce calmed the manager and the police by explaining in Turkish that this was his friend's first visit to Turkey, he was an American, and he knew only three words of Turkish. Calming quickly, the restaurant manager said they'd been offended twice: first by what they perceived as a grossly insulting display of vulgarity (by a foreigner, no less, which doubled the insult), and second, by his having so little respect for Turkish culture that he wouldn't think to bring a $4.95 English-Turkish dictionary to the restaurant with him.

Whoever you select to send overseas must be tested for language aptitude and must above all have an *attitude* that welcomes a foreign language. She must be willing to learn and respect the harsh truth that English is no more the "universal language" than Urdu! Sure, English is the language most widely studied worldwide. But it's also the world's most complex language, boasting the world's largest vocabulary. Furthermore, English is the language in which the most tragic misunderstandings are experienced every single day, in business and in diplomacy. *Because* of its complexity, and *because* so many people in this world know English as a second or even third language, many non-native speakers have weak vocabularies. Which means they have trouble expressing their real wishes and needs.

For many of us, the title of this chapter was a mantra from our mothers. But we sometimes forget this rule from childhood, especially when we send valued staff members into foreign cultures. In this chapter, we focus on something that almost can't be named. Not cultural sensitivity; not the urgent need to learn the language of the land where you'll be working and living; not learning to say things in a manner that won't offend people from other cultures. No. We'll focus on all of these rolled into one—and more.

WHOSE ENGLISH ARE YOU USING?

The British Empire "owned" a huge expanse of our world for more than two hundred years. Hence most overseas cultures are familiar with the English language of Great Britain. Americans tend to speak English with a directness and even strength of tone we find comfortable. But in truth, our tone is offensive in many countries, where people are accustomed to British tone and usage. (Winston Churchill once remarked about the United States and Great Britain, "Two great nations separated by a common language!") That doesn't make the American tone *wrong*, any more than it makes the British tone *right*. But it's an important fact American staff in overseas postings should recognize.

Some years ago, Bruce arranged a meeting in London between a client and one of Britain's foremost financial houses. Against Bruce's advice, the client insisted on bringing his company's vice president for finance along—a man who understood numbers, but who had little sense of either language or cultural differences. Throughout the morning and into lunch—at which some of the most prominent members of the financial house were in attendance, including members of the House of Lords—the VP pressed an aggressive attack, making demands, interrupting, and generally violating every tenet of British business reserve. Finally after several more subtle warnings, one of the hosts turned to him and, with classic British understatement, said, "Sir, you are here at our sufferance." The American VP's immediate response: "Who's suffering? Who said anything about suffering? If anybody's suffering here, it's me!"

Needless to say, the meeting did not go well. A week after returning home, the client received a letter (which we still have) from the financial house indicating that "with suitable regrets," further business would not be possible. The VP's linguistic slips had revealed the truth: whatever financial acumen he might have had was completely undermined by his inability to do business across even a relatively modest cultural gap.

Even the difference in the way *a* is pronounced in the two dialects of the same language can be difficult to understand at first. Americans are well-known for their own adulation for the Queen's English. In a *New Yorker* cartoon a few years back, two bins of tomatoes were shown in a supermarket. One had a sign: TOMATOES— 29¢/LB. The one right beside it said TOMAHTOES—39¢/LB!

Language structures can vary widely as well. In some languages, verb forms are kept very simple. In Afrikaans, for example, *I am, you are, he is* become *ek is, jy is, hy is.* In 1991, in all the chaos that ensued in the former Soviet Union after the collapse of that empire, Bruce was tasked by an American corporate client to bring back to Washington the minister of nuclear energy for Kazakhstan. Vladimir (*vlahd-DEE-meer*) was a towering, outgoing Russian who, though eager to accompany Bruce on the longest trip of his life, spoke not one word of English. So Bruce naturally assumed the role of interpreter and translator for both Vladimir and the client.

On the long flight west, Bruce noticed Vladimir had a remarkable talent for languages. He compelled Bruce to explain the morphology and grammatical structure of English (in Russian) for two solid hours. Once in Washington he checked Vladimir into a nice hotel on Embassy Row, but warned him that Washington was a city with high crime, and he needed to stay put in his luxurious hotel until a driver collected him!

The next day, Bruce and a driver drove to the hotel to collect their guest of honor. You can only imagine the frustration when there was no Vladimir to be found! They waited an hour—then decided that they had to call the local police. Suddenly they saw Vladimir sauntering along toward them, smiling broadly. He appeared to be talking to himself.

Flustered, Bruce asked him where the h*ll he had been. Well, he had walked all the way into the southeast quadrant of the nation's capital—into an area widely known for its exceptionally high crime rate. How had the locals treated him? "Oh," the Russian replied volubly in his newest language, "I likingk much this English they are speakingk there! Much easy! I be, you be, he be!"

RIGHT IDEA, WRONG WORDS

Languages other than English can be subjected to similar sorts of misinterpretations. A few years back, an American airline created "rendezvous lounges" in its business-class section as a way of attracting business customers with an added perk—an area to stretch and gather outside one's seat. They advertised this new feature heavily both in the United States and in Europe, hoping to attract European businessmen coming to the States as well as Americans going abroad. Unfortunately, the airline's marketers failed to note that *rendezvous* in Portuguese refers to an illicit sexual encounter—probably not luring the kind of clientele they were hoping to attract!

Some years back, a married couple (friends of ours) traveled to Paris on business, taking their daughter Mishel as an interpreter. Mishel spoke fluent French and handled their meetings with skill and grace.

Having been warned that Parisians view Americans as a necessary evil, the couple tried to keep a low profile and stay out of trouble. The wife remembered enough French from college to ask for basic things, such as bathrooms, water, and *l'hôtel*. Mastering a few basic words in French and using a polite, formal manner of speaking worked well for the couple. They learned to say, *Bonjour, madame. Parlez-vous anglais?* Thankfully, most Parisians would respond in English and let them off the hook.

After a few days in the city, Mishel put them on the subway (*le métro*) by themselves. They navigated well enough, especially since they were in no hurry and didn't mind getting lost.

The wife watched the other women on the *métro*, marveling at their style. The guidebook in her purse advised, "Check out the latest styles in *Elle* and *Vogue* for an overview of what to wear in Paris." But these women weren't dripping in designer gear. They wore clothes with the knowledge that whatever they had on suited them perfectly. The style was classic and timeless.

Riding on the *métro*, two elegant women in the opposite seat stared openly at them, nudged each other, and whispered. The wife smiled at them. They turned away. American puppy-dog friendliness isn't well accepted in Paris. The wife sensed that Parisian culture is deep and complicated—far more so than they could absorb in a week's time. They later learned the French don't smile as often or readily as Americans, but this doesn't mean they're unfriendly—it's just a cultural difference. At the time, though, the wife felt rejected and buried her nose in a book.

At each stop, new passengers crowded into the seats around them. When the car was full, the couple offered their seats to a pair of elderly ladies. This won a nod of approval and a tiny smile from the two women who'd snubbed them. They realized that kindness and courtesy are universal in any language.

The couple hung on to the metal railing, swaying back and forth with the rhythm of the car. A stern-looking French businessman in a tailored overcoat squeezed in beside them with an apologetic shrug. When the car began moving, he reached for the railing but found no handhold. The husband held out his bright yellow umbrella, which had a handle shaped like a duck's head.

"Here, you can hold my duck!" he announced in French.

The man's face turned pale. Everyone stared at them.

"It was a joke," the wife stammered in English. "Our umbrella looks like a duck." She held it up for all to see, but no one seemed to appreciate the humor. The Frenchman moved a safe distance away and stared out the window.

Later they explained the episode to Mishel, who laughed until she cried. "Dad, you totally blew it! *Duck* is a slang word for *ass* in French. You told the man he could hold your ass!"

C'est la vie! They learned that making jokes—especially puns—in a foreign country is asking for problems.

RIGHT WORDS, WRONG DELIVERY: I'M SORRY, COULD YOU REPEAT THAT?

Sometimes even working in the same language can pose problems. Several years ago Bill had a series of meetings with senior academics at the University of Stellenbosch, one of the finest research institutions in Africa. He met with administrators who had doctorates and significant scholarly credentials, were highly educated, and had a solid command of English. But their native language was Afrikaans. During these conversations, he noticed that if he spoke at a typical American speed, their eyes glazed over. He knew they weren't getting everything he said. When he slowed down the pace a mere half step, their anxiety eased and conversation flowed more smoothly. As simple and subtle a change as a half beat in the pace of language—not "dumbing down" or speaking . . . too . . . slowly . . . with . . . only . . . small . . . words—made all the difference. Had he not done this, the meetings would have accomplished nothing. As it was, they were a success and led to a fruitful partnership that later included faculty and student exchanges and international conferences across several continents. People you send overseas must not only be able to communicate in other languages—they must have command of their *own* language and adapt it to different listeners' needs.

Of course, this can work the other way around. In his younger days, Bruce landed in Helsinki with his boss, many years older. They grabbed a taxi at the airport and headed into central Helsinki. Along the way, the boss spoke derisively and rudely about the large company they planned to visit. The next morning, in the company's elegant boardroom, they were given the cold shoulder—not even offered coffee, which was an unspeakably harsh signal in the Finnish culture. "We understand you actually hold a good deal of contempt for our company, so of course this meeting will be mercifully brief." And it was!

As the two left in disgrace, one of the executives spoke softly to them in the elevator. "It's generally prudent to hold one's tongue in a country in which you are a guest." To their astonishment, he then told them their taxi driver from the day before had a Finnish father but a British mother and hence spoke both Finnish and English with equal fluency. He had been so offended by the boss's remarks that he had driven directly to the company from the hotel and reported the conversation almost verbatim.

Sensitivity to language can also save your people a lot of embarrassment. Anyone who has done business in Japan, for example, knows that *maybe* means "no." It *always* means no. *Very difficult* is even worse. It means "no freakin' way." The Japanese culture's deep respect for civility impels them never to use the word *no* in the forthright way that North Americans are accustomed to hearing.

But business does need to get done in Japan. Moreover, in Japan *personal contact*, up to and including golf matches and saunas with business counterparts, is vital. Understanding the culture, its limits, and having somebody around who speaks the language is vital in negotiations that can sometimes resemble a Kabuki dance.

An associate of ours, an American executive with Asia-wide responsibility, needed to cut costs. His company's longtime Japanese partner was charging about double what he could get elsewhere for the same service. After a year of going through channels and getting nowhere, the American deliberately took a chance. At a get-to-know-you meeting at the American's base in Hong Kong held to introduce a new vice president of the Japanese company, and including a dozen of the Japanese who had been stalling for a year, the American delicately, then less delicately, raised the price issue. Since this was a gross violation of protocol, the Japanese batted the queries away as not appropriate. As the American insisted, without raising his voice, but not giving in, either, an animated discussion broke out among the Japanese, in Japanese.

Unbeknownst to the Japanese, the American company's Norwegian-born, blond, blue-eyed advertising director spoke fluent Japanese. From time to time she'd pass her boss a note saying, "You won't believe what they just called you," or, "They are getting *really* unhappy." This allowed the American to judge when to stop and accept the answer: "We'll study it." Upon their return to Tokyo, the Japanese cut their price in half—to where it should have been all along. Had our colleague's team not had this facility with the Japanese language, the strategy would never have worked.

There's more. Americans tend not only to say too much, but are also extremely nervous with silence. (This is far less true of Canadians, so our Canadian readers can skip this paragraph if they like!) This fact is known and exploited every day by savvy executives of other countries. It might fascinate you to know that a number of serious academic studies on this quirk have been conducted over the years—a couple of them are cited in our bibliography. Americans tend to fill silence with what we call small talk: "How do you like this weather?" "What did you think of the Red Sox last night?" Alas, many non-American cultures not only disdain this kind of small talk, they are actually offended by it. But offended or not, many have learned over the years that if you sit staring (smiling) at an American executive in a business meeting—in complete silence—within about eight seconds the American will start talking! And usually he offers useful information to the other side that he should have kept for a while longer to himself. Our advice: learn how to live with silence in meetings. Practice it deliberately with colleagues. Make sure the people you are sending overseas master this before they leave North America.

A FOR EFFORT: THE REWARDS OF EVEN
A LITTLE LANGUAGE

Language is nothing more than a collection of sounds—and a table of rules for connecting those sounds in a way that presents meaning. But those sounds are important. Americans often wince at the harsh vowels foreign visitors use in speaking English, but they give little thought to how we sound to others when we make no effort to say *ah* instead of the more American-style *a* in *at*.

We tend to make far too much of foreign languages, in the sense that they are "too difficult." Swiss and Dutch children are often raised bi- or trilingually without a second thought to the difficulty. *Difficult* is a relative term and tends to become trivial when we balance it against ability and attitude.

Although making universal claims about world cultures is usually ill-advised, we can state one thing for sure: in forty years of working around the world, we have never found any people that failed to express excitement, warmth, and welcome *just for the attempt to speak a few phrases in their language*. This encouragement serves as a natural stepping-stone to learning the language. The dividends of trust and goodwill one receives for this effort are virtually incalculable.

In an effort to build up foreign sales, a U.S. manufacturer sent to Europe a salesman who knew the business thoroughly and had a proven record in the United States. During his first few years overseas, he performed as expected, and sales orders poured in regularly. But the promising beginning soon turned dark. After a small European company began manufacturing a competitive product, sales plummeted for the American firm. Later analysis showed the American manufacturer's problems lay with the attitudes and role perception of their "man in Europe." He felt that, as the expert, his role was to tell foreign business associates what to do, not to listen to them or seek ways to better satisfy local market needs. (We'll show throughout this book that this is by far the most egregious and common error made by Americans and Canadians overseas—and the most costly and preventable one.) Furthermore, he failed to develop a personal appreciation for the environment in which he lived. After living for seven years in a French-speaking community, he was unable to say or understand *bonjour*, and his superior and indifferent attitude antagonized French distributors. The initial successes for the U.S. firm could be traced to the strength of the product and the lack of competition. But once competition appeared, the U.S. manufacturer suffered at once: even though the competitive product was inferior, the competitor's obliging and positive attitude won over the distributors and swept the market.[1]

Of course, sometimes language barriers can be humorous. Bruce lived for some time in North Carolina. Being fluent in German, he was hosting a small cadre of engineers from Germany, who asked to visit remote areas of the state. Along the way he stopped to refuel the car at a typical combined gas station and country store. The Germans went inside. He waited a long time for them to come out. Too long. Finally he went in to see if there might be a problem. One of the engineers came up instantly, quite flustered. In whispered German he said, "We smile and thanked them, but every time we get to the door, they yell to us, 'Y'all come back now!' So we do!"

It's no secret that many Americans lack the aptitude for languages—and there's no shame in this. Neither of the authors could survive five minutes on a South African rugby pitch. But when an overseas staffer doesn't have this aptitude, all kinds of problems can arise. On a trip to South Africa a few years ago, Bruce had a young but very capable American man with him. The

1. David Ricks et al., *International Business Blunders* (Columbus, OH: Grid, 1974), 57–59.

American was knowledgeable in one particular area and would be introduced to several leaders whose language and culture were Afrikaans. Knowing this young man had little aptitude for languages, we encouraged him to learn two appropriate words for the end of the meeting: *Baie dankie*, which means "thank you very much." This phrase is easy to pronounce and instantly understood by Afrikaans-speaking people. So we taught him: just remember "Buy a donkey!" How hard can that be?

Well, it was too much for this otherwise talented young man. At the end of the meeting, he grasped the hand of the senior-most statesman and spluttered, "Buy a burrito!" Oh, to have had a camera for that moment, and to have captured the stunned looks on their faces! Since Mexican food does somehow make its way around the world, several of the leaders did form a generic mind-picture of a burrito. But none of them could stretch a link between a stuffed tortilla on a plate and this man's—was he thinking of a burro?—words!

As an aid to those of you who are considering going overseas yourselves, we have included a series of phrase guides with pronunciations in the back of this book, in various languages. The list obviously isn't comprehensive. It can't cover every possible phrase, or every language you might be called upon to use. But it gives you a sense of what it takes simply to learn to be polite. If you can master one of these lists—only a few simple phrases—you're on your way to where you need to be. And even using a few of these phrases at key moments can light up a room and spell the difference between warm acceptance and casual indifference.

SUMMARY

Language fear often keeps Americans and Canadians at home: fear of having to learn a new language, fear of being misunderstood, fear of simply being someplace where you can't ask for directions to the bathroom. In business, some of these fears are well-grounded because language *is* important. Getting it wrong can wreck your global business chances, as you've seen from the stories here. But it *is* a manageable issue, if you keep a few key things in mind:

- Just because you're working in English doesn't mean you or your employees will be understood. Understand the different kinds of English at play in your host country.
- Be *very* careful you understand the meanings of words before you use them. This is true in marketing and other materials, but also important to impress upon the people you send.
- *How* your employees use language is almost as important as which language they use. Americans tend to talk too fast and too much. Make sure your people don't make that mistake.
- The language issue is fundamentally about *attitude*. Even if your people have little language skill, making a sincere effort can pay tremendous dividends—and refusing to make that effort can impose serious penalties.

Should your people learn the language to go abroad? Yes, but you won't necessarily have somebody who's fluent in the needed language immediately at hand (though if you do, great!). If it's a long-term assignment, it's something people can work up to—nothing teaches a language like having to use it! But for *all* kinds of assignments, even short trips to hold exploratory meetings, language is a critical issue. The more you approach it professionally, the better the rewards will be.

5

No Missionaries!

IN 1977, A YOUNG man named Michael Maren did what generations of idealistic young Americans have done—he went off to join the Peace Corps. Finding himself in Kenya, where nomadic herdsmen faced annual cycles of wet and dry seasons, he hit on what he thought was the perfect solution to a basic problem: access to water. He would purchase a water locator, drilling equipment, and wind-powered well pumps and go around the plains drilling wells to save the poor Kenyan herders of cattle and sheep from their benighted state. He would be, as he put it, the "Johnny Appleseed of water."

Funding was easy to come by—he found no shortage of donor groups willing to invest in a project based on wind power that would bring the benefits of civilization to these supposedly poverty-stricken people. But before setting off on the quest, he brought his idea to an older, more experienced hand in the area, who explained to Maren that, rather than bringing the basics of civilization to rural Kenyans, Maren's plan would kill them.

The man drew a small circle in the middle of a piece of paper. The circle, he explained, is the well; the paper represents the desert from which Maren was trying to save the Kenyans. In the dry season, Kenyans would bring their animal herds to the well to water them. The animals would begin to graze out the grass around the well. The man drew a second, larger circle—the distance a cow can walk in a day. Since cows need to be watered daily, when all the grass in that circle was gone, the cows would die. He drew a third circle—the distance sheep and goats can walk in several days. Since sheep and goats can last a few days without water, they can go farther, but when this larger circle was denuded of grass, they would die, too. Then he drew a fourth circle for camels. Camels can go a long ways without water, but eventually the distance to food would be too great for them as well, and they, too, would die. Then the Kenyans would die with them.[1]

Maren's story illustrates a basic but little-appreciated truth: things are as they are for reasons. If you don't understand those reasons—if you don't get the underlying forces at work—any attempt to solve a problem may cause greater ones. With foreign cultures in particular, the realities we don't see often get us into trouble. And you can get into some of the worst trouble by sending people abroad who want to change the world.

You may be reading this book not because your organization wants to save starving Kenyans, but because you want to do business. But just because saving the world isn't in your company's mission statement doesn't mean your employees won't try to do it anyway—and even if it *is* in your mission statement, your people may decide to freelance on their own and thus get you into trouble.

---

1. Michael Maren, *The Road to Hell: The Ravaging Effects of Foreign Aid and International Charity* (New York: Free Press, 1997), 9–10.

People tend to have firmly grounded ideas about "the way things are supposed to be." When we encounter differences, we have an instinctive response to try to manipulate them to match our own views.

BUT THAT'S JUST WRONG!
THE UNINTENTIONAL MISSIONARY

Sometimes this instinct to change the world can be unconscious and unintended—but still disastrous. On the first page of this book, you read a dramatic story. Let's review it here. Some years ago, Bruce was on a flight that had just begun descending to the main airport of a major Arab country. The normal hum and chatter of a plane flight was suddenly interrupted by screams. "No way!" a woman shouted at the top of her lungs. "You're not getting that damned thing on me!"

She was a young American woman in her midtwenties. The "thing" was a black cloth chador, the modesty garment worn by Muslim women throughout most of the Islamic world, which she—and other women on the flight not already so attired—had been instructed to put on before arrival.

The crew told the hysterical woman that passing out such garments to Western women before landing was required by national law. But she would have none of it. "You'll be arrested, miss, and probably treated very harshly," the *maître de cabine* warned her in soft tones. "Because not to be covered modestly and properly is considered an offense unto Allah."

All to no avail. After we landed, a heated exchange in Arabic with security police took place at the forward door of the aircraft. Seconds later three officers yanked the woman from her seat and dragged her, still shouting, down the ramp connected to the plane. Bruce was not far behind them, hoping he might help. But it was too late. A representative of the dreaded religious police, or *muta'awa*, joined the party. He lashed at the woman's exposed legs with a small whip, inducing cries and tears.

Within a few hours she had been arrested, released, and placed against her will on a flight to a European city.

Bruce pursued the story. She was a middle-management employee of a large American multinational corporation, on her first overseas assignment. She'd received almost no training about entering an Arab country that was highly orthodox in observing the strictures of Islam. She reacted the way Americans often do—trying to force others to accept her way of doing things, rather than respecting theirs.

Americans and Canadians are trained almost from birth to be "rugged individualists"—to build our own identities. Whether this really happens is irrelevant; this is how many North Americans perceive themselves. The generation now at an age for middle management was raised on *Free to Be . . . You and Me* and *Sesame Street* messages of "be yourself." To the North American mind, no one has the right to tell us how to act, what to wear, or who we can be.

But people you send overseas *must* leave this attitude behind. When you send an employee to represent your company, that person is a guest in a foreign culture. He has no right to insist that his hosts "accept him as he is." Any attempt to force another culture to accept what we in America see as perfectly normal diversity can end in disaster for your company—as the incident with the woman on the plane showed only too well.

A friend of ours had a similar experience—but learned her lesson better than the woman on the plane, and earlier. She was a practicing nurse, visiting Lima, Peru, with a health-care team from an American university, providing health care to Peruvians who did not always enjoy access to it.

While in Lima, she enjoyed wandering through the city. Her Spanish language skills consisted mostly of phrases like *dolor de cabeza* (headache) and *dolor de estómago* (stomachache), but she had for the most part been able to communicate without serious issues.

Tiny neighborhood stores surrounded her hostel in a crowded, nontourist part of Lima. After a few days, she had fallen in love with the friendly people of Peru and felt safe walking the streets alone. She sauntered along in the afternoon sunshine, occasionally pausing to browse in the shops or sit on a bench and people-watch. While doing so, she wore her public nurse's uniform: a below-the-knee skirt topped by a modest cotton blouse.

After a couple of hours of wandering, she found a cool, inviting restaurant and decided to have a soft drink and a sandwich. The dining room bustled with activity, but no one seemed to notice her. After waiting a few minutes at the entrance, she moved into a chair at an empty table. The three Peruvian waiters seemed efficient, yet no one brought her a menu or a glass of water, though patrons at the other tables had silverware, drinks, and food. She fluttered her hand and the nearest waiter shied away, rushing into the kitchen as though she had bubonic plague. How strange! She had been to restaurants in Lima with her group and had never had a problem.

She sat by herself for thirty minutes, then finally moved to another café down the street. The service was equally bad. Sitting alone at a table in the corner, she felt like the invisible woman. Even the other patrons made a point of ignoring her.

Being ignored once could be a fluke, but after striking out twice, she realized the problem was her. Did they not serve foreigners?

What rule had she broken? Snippets of her (too brief) cultural-orientation lecture floated through her brain. What had the instructor said about women? Peru was still a male-dominated society, even in the city.

"Wear skirts and modest clothing. . . . Don't go into a restaurant alone . . . single woman do not dine alone—you'll be seen as a possible prostitute and won't be served. Peruvian women never dine out alone."

Now she understood. They tolerated her—a *gringa*—in the restaurants because the owners were too polite to ask her to leave. Or perhaps they feared she'd make a scene. She could occupy a table, but these local cafés would never serve her.

She stared at the other diners, frustrated. She had traveled to Peru at her own expense to provide free health care, yet these people wouldn't let her eat alone in their restaurants. What kind of hospitality was that? Didn't they know women were equal? Quickly, the missionary impulse rose: how do I show these people that they're wrong?

Then she reconsidered. As a guest in Peru, it wasn't her place to change their culture, test their patience, or impose American values. She gathered her things and left the restaurant before she could further embarrass herself. She got it. But many don't.

MY WAY OR THE HIGHWAY: EMPLOYEES WHO TRY TO CHANGE THE WORLD

The missionary instinct is built on this basic assumption: *my way is the right way*. More times than either of us can count, we've heard traveling Americans overseas ask in shops and restaurants, "How much is that in *real money*?" This may seem like a small thing, but if an employee you're considering sending overseas shows such tendencies, *do not send him*.

Business executives often go abroad after long, successful careers, which leads to the "I know how to do it" syndrome—a recipe for disaster overseas. Several years ago, Bruce was consulting for an American businessman who wanted to arrange a partnership in Hong Kong with a local business. As a necessary step toward a successful business relationship, Bruce arranged a dinner at a nice Hong Kong restaurant. The American client was told, in no uncertain terms, there must be *no* discussion over dinner of any business deals—such a thing would be unthinkable to the Chinese partner he wished to court. For Chinese businessmen, social dinners are a standard part of the courtship of commerce (especially first dinners).

The dinner began as planned and the American client behaved himself—for all of ten minutes. While the meal was still in the hors d'oeuvres stage, the client suddenly announced, "Let's cut the crap and get down to brass tacks." He reached inside his jacket and pulled out a typed business proposal. This man was convinced he knew how to do business and was hell-bent on showing this poor Chinese businessman how it *should* be done.

Not only did the deal fall through, but Bruce never recovered the friendship of the Chinese billionaire. He had extended courtesy and cordiality but was deeply insulted and (wrongly) believed we hadn't briefed our client. That's another expensive lesson about such faux pas: things often never recover to where they were. You can lose a lot in five minutes.

Have you seen the 1980 film *Dogs of War*, starring Christopher Walken and Tom Berenger? It's the screen version of the Frederick Forsyth novel of the same title. The film is about a group of brutal mercenaries paid by corporate interests to overthrow the government of a small African country and to install a government more friendly to Western corporate interests. It's fiction. But on a steamy Sunday evening in March 2004, a privately owned 727 set down at the Harare airport in Zimbabwe to pick up a cargo from Simon Mann, a British citizen residing in Cape Town, South Africa.

The plane never left again. Zimbabwean troops surrounded the plane and its strange group of passengers. They were charged with attempting to buy weapons from the state-run Zimbabwe Defense Industries. Their arms requisition included 20 machine guns, 61 assault rifles, 150 hand grenades, 10 rocket-propelled grenade launchers (with 100 RPG shells), and 75,000 rounds of ammunition. They claimed they were going to the Democratic Republic of the Congo to protect diamond mines under contract. But in truth they had been paid handsomely by a consortium of British companies to invade and overthrow the government of Equatorial Guinea. This debacle shamed and ruined the career of Lady Thatcher's son, Mark. This was a modern *Dogs of War* (which phrase comes from act 3, scene 1, of Shakespeare's play *Julius Caesar*: "Cry 'Havoc!' and let slip the dogs of war").

This recent story is an extreme example of improper meddling in local affairs. The event not only gripped much of Africa during the trial, but you can also be certain it soured African governments toward Western companies for many years to come, instilling distrust where trust is needed. (We'll talk more about this kind of meddling, and the trouble it can get your organization into, in chapter 9.)

Even on a local level, meddling by your employees can be dangerous and get your company thrown out of a country forever. On a personal level, meddling can get your employees hurt or killed. The record is sound on this; the examples from history are many. In short, keep the missionaries at home. There's a reason that one of the most popular sayings in Africa is "God save us from missionaries!"

Spouses sometimes get in on the act. Your company may choose wisely and give your envoy the best available orientation and information. But what about the trailing spouse who's likely to have a lot of time on her hands? Companies have less control over family members once the family moves overseas, so consider carefully before making a choice.

A leading pharmaceutical company sent a talented senior executive to run its affairs in a rather sophisticated African country. He did stellar work there. But his spouse was a self-anointed missionary. Within a few months, she had agitated locals of all races with her zealous pursuit of "changing things to be more American." The company's head of security in the United States had to rush to the scene to quell the intrusion and secure a pledge from the woman that she would stop interfering. Fortunately, the head of security was able to dampen local press interest. Otherwise, the company's sales in that market would have suffered gravely. People in other countries vehemently dislike having their affairs and interests disrespected by foreigners.

KILLING WITH KINDNESS: THE DANGERS OF BEING CHARITABLE

But surely, you might say, a little charity work can't hurt? Helping the locals is one way companies make a good name for themselves, as most major corporations in America and Canada know. But overseas, "contributions" with the best of intentions can make things worse, not better, and because you're working in a foreign environment, mistakes are easy to make.

A striking number of American celebrities—brand names in themselves—have gotten involved in "charitable" work in Africa in recent years, and many have come to regret it. In early 2007, Oprah Winfrey opened a Leadership Academy for Girls outside Johannesburg in South Africa. The $40 million complex featured state-of-the-art facilities and luxuries—including a yoga studio and hair salon—that the girls, many of them from poor townships, had never dreamed of. Winfrey herself visited the opening and made much of her efforts on her widely syndicated North American TV show.

But building schools for Third World poor is not like giving cars to middle-class Americans in your studio audience. The school has been dogged by controversy over the treatment of parents, restrictions placed on children to prevent them from seeing their families, and allegations of sexual and physical abuse (with one school employee currently on trial in South Africa). The South

African media suggested that the school's location—in Henley-on-Klip, the Beverly Hills of South Africa—says more about the founder's tastes than about concern for the poor who live in Soweto. The result has not been an outpouring of support for the celebrity's business empire, but a source of constant questions, scandals, and negative publicity. From now on, all of Winfrey's activities in Africa will be scrutinized. Trying to change the world and failing—as efforts abroad usually do—is bad for business.

South Africa has an interesting system of pay called the "thirteenth check." (Variations of this occur in Belgium and other countries, too.) Essentially it is a bonus check (an extra month's pay) that is given to employees just in advance of Christmas, so they can cover the expenses of Christmas. It is a cultural expectation that goes back more than a century. One of the reasons for this is that pay levels in South Africa are not at Western levels, especially for unskilled labor. While Bruce was living in South Africa, he received a call one day from a South African manager he knew. The woman was frantic and asked if Bruce would come "sort out" the American CEO who had just been hired to take over a factory on the Indian Ocean side of South Africa.

When Bruce arrived, he was not surprised to find the CEO cordial but adamant: "This is a stupid practice, and I refuse to endorse it! So I've canceled it. And now they won't work! But I'm going to make them accept the much more sensible American practice of *earning* their bonuses!" You mean the sensible American practice of giving gargantuan bonus checks to executives whose companies have actually experienced annual losses? Or the practice of giving obscene bonuses to salesmen who actually had not even come close to their sales targets? It took Bruce more than hour to calmly persuade the American CEO that one does *not* simply march into another country and disrespect their practices. South Africa is the most developed country of Africa's fifty-four nations—it is quite advanced in business practices. Its millions of employees depend on that thirteenth check as part of their livelihoods. To cancel the practice was also interpreted by the workers as a blatant judgment of their worth to the company.

Not surprisingly, even when the workers did agree to resume work (after the CEO announced that the thirteenth check would be reinstated), their attitudes were dark. The I'll-show-them-how-it's-done attitude of the inexperienced American CEO had destroyed the most valuable of all virtues in a company: trust. The employees no longer trusted him. More than a year later, managers told Bruce, "This place will never again be the same. He's broken our spirit." Before you start to "do good," take the trouble and the humility to find out what the locals consider to *be* good.

SUMMARY

Businesses don't usually send people overseas because they want to save the world; they send people because they want to do business. That's fine, and business, properly done, benefits *all* sides. But sometimes your employees may have agendas other than simply your business—whether they are aware of them or not. You need to be careful, in selecting people to send abroad, that they do not wreck your business in their zeal to fix something else or accomplish some other goal. In particular, keep these things in mind:

- Westerners often react badly to different ways of doing things and may respond by trying to change the locals rather than adapting themselves. Make sure you are sending people who will adapt instead of instinctively trying to "fix" their hosts.
- Employees, or their spouses, may have agendas on how things should be or how they should get done. If the person you're considering has a "missionary" bent and wants to change the world, *don't send him.*

- Charity work overseas can often come across as condescending or send the wrong message about your company. Be *very* careful about trying to "help" the host community—or stick to your business and help by being a good employer and providing goods and services that are wanted.

We'll repeat something here that we said first in chapter 3 and that will come up again: to get this right and avoid the mistakes we've pointed out here, you've got to *know your employees*. People all have many facets; as a rule in American and Canadian businesses, we only let ourselves deal with a narrow slice of those. Get to know your people so you have a sense of whether they are adaptable or whether they carry ideas and agendas that will demand they try to change their hosts. Make sure you're sending effective businesspeople, not missionaries!

6

It's 8 AM Somewhere

IN 1956, EGYPTIAN LEADER Gamal Abdel Nasser's biggest priority was building the Aswan High Dam to provide electricity to the Egyptian economy. The United States and Britain had offered to finance the project, hoping to edge Soviet influence out of Egypt and bring the mercurial Nasser closer to the American side in the Cold War. But in May 1956, Nasser angered his would-be financiers by recognizing the People's Republic of China. In response, on June 19, U.S. secretary of state John Foster Dulles withdrew the American offer of financing on the dam project in the most humiliating fashion possible—not by admitting retaliation for Egypt's flirtation with the communist bloc, but by calling into question Egypt's willingness to repay the loan, thereby insulting Egyptian national honor. In response, Nasser nationalized the Suez Canal, touching off a war involving Egypt, Britain, France, and Israel, which killed over eighteen hundred soldiers on all sides.

Late in his life, Dulles admitted that his withdrawal of the financing offer had been harsh, and that he might have been more conciliatory with the Egyptians—*had he not been suffering from extensive jet lag from his travels.*[1]

Most time-zone crossings don't start wars. But the problems of managing time and time differences around the world create all kinds of problems for businesses, from jet-lagged employees to broken communications between different branches of the company, to ruined meetings, to severe misunderstandings. International business is plagued with problems of time. To be successful, businesses have to understand these problems and make sure that the people they send overseas can adapt to them.

WHAT TIME IS IT HERE? THE PERILS OF JET LAG

Of the time problems associated with travel, jet lag is probably the most recognized, but many people ignore it. Hiram Fong, the first Asian-American ever elected to the U.S. Senate, retired after his third term at least in part because the jet lag from his dozens of flights from D.C. to Hawaii (across six time zones) was taking too great a toll. Greg Louganis, one of the most decorated Olympic divers in history, hit his head on a platform at the 1979 Olympic qualifying meet and attributed his error to the jet lag he suffered flying to Moscow.

Yet people in business—especially from American and Canadian companies used to punctuality and trying to justify the dollars spent sending them overseas—routinely plan their schedules as if jet lag didn't exist. The results can be devastating to business: representatives routinely fall asleep during meetings or while riding in

1. From Charles Ehret, *Overcoming Jet Lag* (New York: Berkeley Trade, 1987), 16.

a client's car, snore through important business dinners, miss meetings by sleeping in, and risk serious injury by stepping off a curb at the wrong moment. Bruce experienced this early in his international career when his employer sent him to Europe to attend a key meeting in Geneva. A Soviet delegation was presenting an important proposal that could at that time have meant some significant advances for Bruce's employer. They relied on him to assess the presentation (which was given in Russian) and report back in detail that day. The flight was not only the traditional all-night "red-eye" flight to Europe; it left three hours late from JFK because of snow. (How many of *you* sleep well on planes, by the way?) Remember, this was early in his career, so he had not yet learned and mastered some of the tricks to minimize the effects of jet lag. His attention dampened by the long night and the six time zones, let's just say that the assignment was not his best performance! Jet lag is not a joke.

But jet lag *is* a simple problem, well studied and well understood. It happens when our internal body clocks get out of sync with our external surroundings because we've crossed several time zones. One typical effect: our brain and stomach think it's three in the afternoon when it's really ten at night. Advice on dealing with jet lag abounds. Sadly, little of it is correct. A few stratagems that do work include: set your watch to the destination time zone the moment you sit down in the plane and start *thinking* right away in your new time zone (the one you're flying to). Stay well hydrated, but with little alcohol. At your destination, get lots of exposure to sunlight outdoors. Be sure not to sleep at your new destination unless you arrive at night and the locals are sleeping then, too. In other words, as soon as you arrive, start on the local schedules, including sleeping and eating the appropriate meals. *Avoid thinking back to what time it* really *is at home—this is a costly mistake, as it delays your adjustment in your new location!* Above all, make absolutely sure that you have no meetings or work scheduled on the day of your arrival. This is easy if you plan ahead and use discipline. And lastly, take a walk. This not only adjusts your body to your new locale (including the local air pressure and humidity, which both influence your circadian rhythms), it also helps your body compensate for the terribly dry air of the long flight you just endured and is believed to minimize any chance of thrombosis in your legs, a common effect of long, cramped flights.

However, some people are much more strongly affected by jet lag than others. Bill has flown seven time zones east and five west, covering half the globe, and rarely feels any significant effects. Bruce has been around the world countless times and in both directions for forty years. Some of his well-proven tricks we shared with you above. Most work very well for him, but now and then he will feel a day's loss. (By the way, it is well established that jet lag is exacerbated by age, so don't feel you're "losing it" if you start to notice yourself feeling more pronounced effects as the years move on. It's completely normal.) Some people need much more structure in their schedule than others. If you have an employee who needs to have meetings at nine o'clock in the morning sharp, do *not* put him on a plane to go twelve time zones west and then schedule a 9 AM meeting!

WHAT TIME IS IT THERE? MANAGING ACROSS TIME ZONES

The United States is pretty much the only country on earth that insists on using the confusing twelve-hour time system and the annoying AM/PM abbreviations. If you're being sent overseas—either on long-term assignment or just for regular business-related travel—learn the twenty-four-hour time system now. It's very easy. See the material in the back of the book. Some call it military time because all military forces in the world use it, including American and Canadian. The system removes confusion. You know right away that 0400 (or 0400h) is four o'clock in the morning. It can never be four in the afternoon because that's expressed as 1600h. The system starts with 0100h to denote the first hour after midnight, then simply goes straight through the next twenty-three hours, adding 1 to each hour. So noon is 1200h, 1 PM is 1300h, and so on. This system also makes it easy to see how much time separates any two time zones.

The problems of jet lag are exacerbated when colleagues or management in the home office *aren't* jet-lagged, but are trying to work from several time zones away. Most international companies run into this problem sooner or later. Employees need to be managed, coworkers need to collaborate, different departments need to work together and provide their input on the same project. Doing this without creating serious problems is a real challenge.

Some of the problems are simply obvious. Looking up time-zone differentials isn't difficult—we've included a handy pullout card at the end of this book (along with a helpful Web site that lets you instantly find the overlapping times when you and your HQ will be able to talk conveniently, when it is daylight in both areas, even if one of you is in the next day!)—but it is remarkable how often it doesn't happen. A college professor being moved by a relocation company across several time zones once received a phone call from the company informing him that the movers would be at his home at 0800h the following morning, and that they would need to be paid by cashier's check. Unfortunately, the call came in to the professor at 1900h—too late to get to a bank or manage a financial transaction. Because it was still business hours at the company's headquarters, nobody there had bothered to think about the time differential, causing a serious problem for their client. Bruce long ago lost count of how many times he has been awakened in the middle of the night in other countries by well-intentioned staff who just could not get their brains around this concept of time-zone spread. If you're entering the international arena—or are assigned to work with people who are—you've got to master this. It's not hard.

Much has been written about the power of technology to solve these problems. E-mail, voice over Internet (VOIP), and Web conferencing have all been suggested as ways for companies to save travel dollars, reduce wear and tear on their employees, and productively manage work teams across multiple time zones. Obviously, these technologies *are* tremendously useful and can even bolster productivity, if work can be handed from team to team sequentially, so that one team works and delivers its product while the other sleeps, handing projects back and forth in a twenty-four-hour cycle that keeps everyone busy during their own daylight hours. But technology also has its limits in overcoming these problems.

Several years ago, Bill was working with a university that had a strong partnership with another institution eight time zones away. The home institution had invested substantial sums of money into a video-conferencing system that could be linked by satellite to its partner, allowing real-time communication that could, it was hoped, lead to jointly taught classes and other academic collaborations. The system received a test when a vendor came to the university wanting to pitch a product that it claimed would help the collaboration. This necessitated a simultaneous meeting—the perfect opportunity to test the technology! Unfortunately, it immediately became clear that the only time when such a meeting could be held was at 0800h for the home campus, which would be 1600h for the overseas partner. This required substantial rearrangements of teaching and meeting schedules, and when the meeting was eventually held, it did not go well—participants on the home end were still waking up and getting into the rhythm of the day, while those on the far end were about ready to break for home. The vendor, having no sensitivity for this difference, charged ahead with an hour-and-a-half presentation that tired and bored both sides. Needless to say, no sale was made.

A company must also be willing to adjust its sense of reality to accommodate time zones or it can end up paying dearly. Some years ago Bruce was international operations manager for a U.S.-based company. The firm was on the cusp of winning a multimillion-dollar deal with a Middle Eastern government—a lucrative sale. The client country was seven hours ahead of the eastern standard time zone of the United States—almost an entire working day. The client required a long technical response to a question, and the ability of Bruce's company to win the sale the next day was predicated on the client's receiving a complete response then and there. But it was after hours and the usual bevy of office staff had gone home. So Bruce sat down that night at about 1900h at the company's telex machine, laboriously preparing one of those infamous five-level "poked" paper tapes that was the world's means of international communication until the fax machine came along in 1987. The company president happened along and asked Bruce what he was doing. Upon hearing the response, he sniffed, "That's what we have secretaries for! Managers do not prepare telexes!" Even when Bruce protested that the seven-hour time differential made it mandatory that this response be prepared and sent that very evening, the president made it quite clear that his word was law. The company lost the sale the next day to a French competitor.

Managing time-zone differences gets even more complicated when you get outside of the North American and European context. Americans and Canadians are used to a certain time-zone range between their east and west coasts, and Europe adheres to more or less the same system of time zones arranged in one-hour blocks divided by north-south lines of longitude. But around the world, time zones can be a mess. India, nearly two thousand miles from east to west, would naturally be divided into two time zones, but it splits the difference on the half hour and keeps the whole country on the same time. Afghanistan does the same (but one hour to the west), while Pakistan sticks to the standard on-the-hour formula, meaning it's a half hour off Afghanistan one way and a half hour off India the other. And Kazakhstan, much of which is due north of India, is an hour and a half off Indian time!

All of this gets more complicated when a company is trying to "do the right thing" in terms of staying in touch with clients and vendors. Ace Greenberg is famous for having established a simple standard when he was chairman of Bear Stearns in the 1990s: all phone calls had to be returned as quickly as possible, period— "even if the person is selling malaria," he once wrote. This is not impossible to do across multiple time zones—but it does take discipline not to let time differences become an excuse for not getting back to people promptly.

Stories abound of expatriates forced to work thirteen-hour days to stay current with both their local time and the home office, or creatively inventing hybrid schedules that allow for overlaps with both local and distant work schedules. Overworking is certainly tempting. One American manager new to Hong Kong and temporarily without his family began his assignment by working 0900h (Hong Kong time) to 1900h, grabbing some dinner, then getting on e-mail in his hotel room. New York was just waking up, so he'd start e-mailing or telephoning with the home office. The first couple of nights he didn't look up from his screen until 0500h, a couple hours before he needed to wake up for the next day's work. This lasted four days, before he swore off e-mail in the evenings.

These problems can be exacerbated if the field office is expected to cover a wide range of territory (companies will sometimes locate a "Europe office" in Berlin or Amsterdam, for example, necessitating travel around the Continent), and especially if it is not as heavily staffed as the home office is—which is frequently the case. Employees sent overseas can find themselves traveling much more extensively than they would in a comparable position in their home country, with less support, and under communications demands from people who don't always know where the overseas employees are—or who may not bother to check ahead of time.

Headquarters-based managers may be tempted to solve these

problems with an easy-looking solution: find people to send overseas who don't need much supervision, and then don't communicate with them much. The first part of this is almost certainly essential. If you send someone who needs constant guidance, all of the time-zone and communication issues we've raised here are going to play havoc with the assignment and ensure rapid failure. But the second part is almost certainly a huge mistake. In any good organization, important conversations will be going on back at the central office that your person in the field will need to be in on. Management's job is to figure out which conversations those are, and to work to keep the field person tied into them.

For this, communications technology *is* tremendously valuable. As we've pointed out, teleconferences and other synchronized, at-the-same-time communications can be problematic, especially if done frequently, but *asynchronous* tools are particularly helpful. Anything that can be sent, read, or received at leisure on the other end, then replied to in their time, can help get this done. E-mail is probably the best tool here: it's instantaneous, it doesn't require the receiver to be there when it comes in, and it allows for measured responses that fit into the receiver's schedule.

Which conversations do your field people need to know about? Could you create and send to them a brief memo with a short synopsis of these? Could you, when they send their feedback, make sure those get distributed to the people who need to see it? None of this takes a tremendous amount of managerial time or talent, but it will help your people overseas do *their* jobs better.

Managing all of these pitfalls across time zones calls for particular skills in the people you send abroad that probably have little to do with the jobs they're being sent to do. First and foremost is *flexibility*. People who need predictable routines that don't vary from day to day are likely to wilt under these kinds of conditions. The ability to translate time zones in one's head—similar to knowing a foreign language—is also key. (Using the 24-hour time system makes this easier.) To be successful overseas, the people you send have to have an intuitive and instantaneous grasp of time differences, and the ability to adjust their communications and work practices to match the demands of the moment. This is similar to fluency in language and cultural sensitivity and is every bit as important.

TIMES ARE CHANGIN': TIME IN DIFFERENT CULTURES

Lots of writing on expatriate qualifications includes some notion of cultural adaptability. As we have said elsewhere in this book, if you can't learn to bow or eat different foods or learn a few phrases of another language, you don't belong in the international arena. But we often assume, without thinking about it, that while we expect language and food and greeting customs to be different, other cultures also handle time the same way we do. This mistake makes the characteristic of time adaptability doubly important.

Years ago, Bruce had to fly from Istanbul to Lisbon to meet with a client. The flight into Lisbon ended up badly delayed, and by the time he reached the hotel, he was tired and strung out from what should have been a simple cross-continental journey. He had also had nothing to eat for many hours. It was nearly midnight as he stumbled into the hotel's restaurant, which was largely deserted. After a few minutes of his staring into empty space, a waiter came along on some errand. Bruce explained that he had had a long and difficult day, had just arrived at the hotel, and would very much appreciate it if they could make an exception and come up with something for him to eat. The waiter looked at him sympathetically for a moment, then replied, "Well, sir, you're a little bit early, but I'm sure we can accommodate you!" *Muito obrigado!*

The Portuguese are hardly alone in sharing a sense of daily schedules vastly different from Americans' typical six-o'clock dinnertime. Families in Saudi Arabia routinely gather at midnight or later for dinner—the best time of day to escape the scorching heat of the desert sun. Beaches for kilometers in all directions in Jidda, Saudi Arabia, are alight with huge fires built to cook the families' meats. Many Americans are familiar with the sacred hour of British teatime, but few are used to eating meals in the middle of the night. Meal schedules that differ from the typical American breakfast-lunch-dinner routine can make us feel even more out of place—on top of the jet-lag issues discussed above, which often throw our systems off to begin with.

It is not just *when* meals are eaten that can vary, but *how*. A few years ago, Bill attended a conference on Cyprus, an eastern-Mediterranean island country whose population (in the portion where the conference was held) is mostly ethnically Greek. The conference was on European Union expansion and featured a sizable number of northern-European and American speakers in addition to Greek Cypriots. The conference program was accordingly very European, starting promptly around 0830h and following a schedule familiar to any conference-goer in America, ending around 1730h in the afternoon. To the surprise of some, the hosts actually stuck closely to this schedule.

But at the end of the first full day, after the formally programmed events, the anticipated schedule suddenly vanished. There was to be a dinner for the invited speakers, a seafood meal considered a high mark of the local culture. The schedule had said something vague about "1800h travel to dinner." But after the final session had ended at 1730h, the cultural clock shifted. The guests milled around and talked while the hosts disappeared to do this and that, periodically returning to promise that we would soon be leaving for the restaurant. It was closer to 2000h than 1800h when the guests finally got there, and by then we were famished.

Once there, the guests were treated to a classic Greek *mezze*, a meal with many courses. Bill had luckily been warned of this ahead of time, or he might have done what many hungry Americans would do after having their dinner delayed for two hours at the end of a busy day: seize upon the first substantive dish presented and eat it heartily. But a *mezze* is meant to be a slow dining experience, with many courses of food—we had well over a dozen—presented in a leisurely fashion, one by one. The idea is to eat a little of this and a little of that. The food was delightful, a wonderful selection of fish, cuttlefish, calamari, and other seafood delicacies. But anybody who did not pace himself—as a few of his American colleagues did not—found himself quickly stuffed, then forced to sit through another two hours while food continued past him, one dish at a time. It was probably 2330h before the guests left, and they had not eaten substantially more in that three and a half hours than a typical American or Canadian business diner might in less than half that time.

Weekly schedules can differ as much as daily schedules. Expatriates sent to Saudi Arabia discover that the Western weekend has no relevance there; the whole country shuts down on Fridays, and a Thursday-Friday "weekend" is extremely common. Employees overseas can suddenly find themselves at odds with colleagues or managers at home, who wonder why they are playing tennis on a "workday," or why they insist on sending work-related e-mails on the traditional Saturday-Sunday weekend.

This problem extends to differing cultural perceptions of time and work, too. In many non-Western cultures, activities that look like "social time" to Canadians or Americans are when work actually gets done. Across Europe, long professional meals are quite normal (as Bill discovered in the eastern Mediterranean), while in Japan, employees and professional collaborators often eat together after hours, when a lot of important work gets done. Anybody who wants cooperation from local traditional authorities in Africa had better be ready to sit down for a leisurely drink, if not a meal, before "getting down to business."

Some of these different practices stem from something we often don't see: different cultures see time very differently and treat it in different ways. Jokes about meetings where Germans are punctual to the minute, while southern Europeans saunter in a half hour late, are common. But these differences are real and can often cause unintended consequences.

Consider this story. A guy named David grows up in the United States. As a small boy, his parents always had a car. Everyone he knows has a car and has had access to one since the age of eighteen. With a few exceptions here and there, car ownership is a staple of American life. As a result, David's sense of distance and time is a function of his upbringing. Twenty miles is nothing! Just hop in the car and go! Even when he visits a city in the United States in which he has no car, he can usually get where he needs to go by way of reliable public transportation. Twenty miles? It's no big deal—that's a half hour or so, maybe forty-five minutes.

Then there's Oleg. He lives in a place where traveling twenty miles is a pretty big deal, especially late in the evening, when the buses or trains don't run often. Car ownership is uncommon and public transportation unreliable, so such a trip can be difficult, time-consuming, expensive—or even dangerous! Oleg doesn't "just hop in the car." Never. A twenty-mile trip will likely take hours, and two such trips would consume an entire day.

Now, imagine that David and Oleg are working together on a project. When David asks Oleg to travel twenty miles to the office or to home or to get dinner, he's thinking it's no big deal and doesn't provide any options or opportunity for discussion. But when Oleg hears the request, he's thinking, "How in the world am I supposed to do that? That'll take all day and well into the night!" Since there is no opportunity for discussion, Oleg manages the best he can, but the project slows down and the staff gets more and more grumpy due to David's apparent unreasonableness. Oleg and his team don't know that David isn't being inconsiderate on purpose. In the end the problem can be solved with a few extra dollars in the budget for late-night cab fare, and a willingness to schedule as few meetings as possible, but it might not get discussed until it has become a crisis.[2]

Or here's a real-life example of cross-cultural time differences in business. An unfortunate American manager was working in a South Pacific nation. He hired local natives without considering the island's traditional status system. By hiring too many of one group, he threatened to alter the balance of power among the people. The islanders discussed this unacceptable situation and independently developed an alternative plan. Their discussion took them until 0300h—a common practice in that part of the world. But since time of day was not important to them for when they conducted business in their culture, they saw no reason to wait until morning to present their suggestions to the American. They casually went to his place of residence, but their arrival at such a late hour made him panic. Since he could not understand their language and could not imagine that they would want to discuss business at 0300h, he assumed they were coming to riot and called in the marines! It was some time before the company was able to get back to "business as usual."[3]

Rigorous studies have confirmed what many have long suspected, but usually don't say for fear of "stereotyping": some cultures are much more past- and present-oriented than those of Americans, Canadians, and Europeans, who tend to be focused on the future.[4] Studies have confirmed that native Africans, for

---

2. This story is taken from David Nixon, "Language Barriers, Culture Gaps, and Time Warps: Challenges Managing Globally Diverse Virtual Teams," *Casual Connect Magazine*, Summer 2008.

3. David A. Ricks, *Blunders in International Business* (Malden, MA: Blackwell Publishers, 1999), 7.

4. Charles Hampden-Turner and Fons Trompenaars, *Riding the Waves of Global Culture: Understanding Diversity in Global Business* (New York: McGraw-Hill, 1997).

example, differ significantly from Europeans in their view of structured routines and are generally less amenable to the kind of organized time management that drives most Western businesses. These effects can be overcome with education and experience, but they are an important starting point in determining whom you work with and how—a topic we will discuss in a couple of chapters. Even within Europe, studies have found pronounced differences between cultures in terms of their time orientation: Germans and Swiss tend to be more future-oriented than French, who are more so than Poles, for example.

What all of this suggests is that employees sent overseas need to have not only cultural and linguistic adaptability—as discussed in earlier chapters—but adaptability in time as well. They must be able to understand different time frames and different ways of seeing time—probably one of the hardest things to do in cultural adaptation. This doesn't mean they have to *accept* alternative time frames or bend their business practices to the point where the business no longer functions. In the end, most American and Canadian businesses are based on a Western notion of time— schedules exist and must be met, and future goals are planned. But going overseas and assuming that everyone around you understands this—just because you have understood it since the third grade—is a recipe for failure.

SUMMARY

What does all of this say about the kinds of employees you should be looking for? You hear a lot about "flexibility" in sending people overseas, and that's true. But flexibility isn't a single attribute, like height. *Particular kinds* of flexibility are needed to succeed in the global arena.

First, no matter how much "virtual management" your company tries to do, people will have to travel, even if only for short periods. Indeed, lots of short jaunts back and forth can be harder to manage than simply relocating for months at a time. Whichever your company is doing, you need to have employees who are well versed in travel and can withstand jet lag relatively easily. If they are hard-hit—and some people can get laid out for days—you need to allow for that time in their travel schedule and not assume that flying to Moscow is the same as flying to Chicago. This is where experience matters as well—you don't want to find out that somebody is particularly susceptible to jet lag by flying them overseas for the first time and sending them right off the plane to a client meeting!

Likewise, people have got to be able to *think across time zones*. If you have someone who constantly forgets that San Francisco is three hours behind New York, or who has to look it up every time—that might not be the best person to send halfway around the world. And anybody who's going to operate at that distance for any length of time has got to be extremely adaptable in his daily schedule. The times of *everything*—meetings, office hours, meals, bedtimes, workdays—will be different and may not stay stable from day to day.

Finally, you've got to have someone who is culturally adaptable enough to *understand*—though not necessarily acquiesce to—other views of time. This is particularly true if the person you are sending overseas is going to be managing people from the local culture. Finding ways to adapt work so that the work gets done while accommodating local sensibilities about time is a challenge that some managers will take well to—and others will find completely impossible.

To briefly summarize:

- Make sure that people you send overseas aren't going to be flattened by jet lag. Give them enough time to recover; don't expect them to be productive right off the plane!

- Manage sensibly across time zones. Don't call at 0300h. And don't expect your overseas people to be available during *your* business hours all the time.
- Make sure that the people you send can adapt to different ways of viewing time. Time means *very* different things in different cultures.

7

I Can't Ask *That*!

WE'VE SPENT THE PREVIOUS four chapters talking about what kinds of characteristics are important to success in overseas assignments and international business. We've gone beyond the obvious and commonly argued points—be flexible, understand other cultures—in the service of pointing out a very important truth: *not everybody can do this*. Despite companies' tendency to think otherwise, not everybody will be successful in Copenhagen just because he or she did well in Calgary. No magic, single thing guarantees success. The world is a complex place. It would be surprising if we didn't need complex abilities to deal with it.

By now you may be thinking, "Okay, now what? I'm starting to get the picture of what an internationally successful person looks like. How do I take that picture and apply it to the real world?" In the popular jargon, what's the "practical take-home message" here?

This chapter is where we start to make that connection—where we start to talk less about what the ideal international employees look like and more about how they should get selected, what they should and shouldn't be expected to do, and what kind of constraints the rest of the world will place on them. There's a lot here for both managers and human-resources professionals looking to send people overseas, and for prospective expatriates who think they might want to work abroad. This chapter, though helpful to both, is primarily directed at the managers and HR folks.

HUMAN RESOURCES: THE CRITICAL PLAYER

We can already hear the groans at this subheading. But wait a minute. Human resources tends, more often than not, to be either an ignored office that handles administratively trivial tasks and paperwork, or the butt of jokes from office banter to Scott Adams's *Dilbert* cartoons (though he's none too fond of management, either). But we're going to make a contrarian argument here: human resources needs to play a critical role in what we're going to talk about in this chapter.

The reason is simple. What we're going to describe below—the key elements of a process by which you go about choosing your people most qualified for overseas assignments—is something that most line managers aren't well equipped to do. Managers need to understand the goals and issues they're working on. They devise strategies. They worry about, well, management. Their primary purpose is to get the job done. Often, this involves deciding who's going to do what, which is why we hope managers are reading this book, too—to help them better make those decisions. But as may be clear by now—and will definitely be clearer below—those decisions are not based on how well you know the technical field or the business goals. They're based on *what you know about your people*.

This is where HR can and should play a key role. Arnold Kanarick, who headed HR at the The Limited and Bear Stearns, pointed out, "HR isn't about being a do-gooder. It's about how do you get the best and brightest people and raise the value of the firm." There's an assumption here: that your HR office is primarily concerned with contributing to the organization's goals—which, in this case, means success internationally. And, to be fair, HR practitioners who value their craft are good at this. They're trained professionals who do know how to evaluate aspects of a company's or an organization's people in a way that can assist tremendously in choosing the right people to send overseas.

To do that—to really make a difference in the organization's international success—requires recognizing a fundamental reality: the world is a *very* complex place that does not lend itself to packaged solutions. The primary challenge, as you've already seen and will see again, is finding people who can deal with *differences*— but what kinds of differences vary widely, depending on where your organization wants to go and what it wants to do. As we point out below, there are no simple tests or easy systems for scanning personnel files.

The most important element in selecting people is *knowing who they are*. This goes beyond résumés and personnel files. It involves getting to know people in terms of the dimensions and characteristics of international success discussed in the previous four chapters and outlined on the next page. And it means matching that knowledge to the demands of a particular overseas job or assignment. That's a lot to ask a line manager to do by herself. Human resources can, and should, be a key facilitator of these conversations. We hope you'll see it that way as well.

PORTRAIT OF INTERNATIONAL SUCCESS

So what should you be looking for? By now, you've got a pretty good profile of what a potentially successful overseas assignee should look like. Key characteristics include:

- *Matching demographic characteristics* (gender, race, religion) to the place they're being sent. Different cultures react differently to different sorts of people. Are you sending the right person *for this culture?*

- *Open-mindedness toward difference.* Can the people you're sending work well with others who are different? Do they harbor prejudices toward certain groups or react badly to certain ideas about the world? Sending a male chauvinist to northern Europe and sending a feminist who reacts badly to traditional views of women's roles in business to the Middle East may be equally disastrous choices.

- *Language facility.* People who have no facility whatsoever for learning foreign languages—or, worse still, who actively resist even a modest attempt—should not be sent overseas. Attitude here is as important as skill—language is a lot easier to learn with the right attitude.

- *Language assumptions.* Anyone who thinks the world speaks English, or that the world *ought* to speak English, should stay at home. But people you send should also be discreet enough to realize that anybody around them *could* speak English, so don't use it as a "secret code" just because you're in a foreign land!

- *Acceptance of the world as you find it.* Usually, people adopt customs in other cultures for a reason. You may not agree with their reasons, but trying to change the customs almost always leads to disaster. Anyone infected with the desire to westernize other parts of the world will definitely do a poor job of representing your business. You don't have to *like* everything you find, just don't make it your mission to change it.

- *Tolerance of different ways of doing business.* There's a balance between going along with the local ways and being effective. Sometimes, foreign business customs really do get in the way of getting things done. But somebody sent overseas must make every effort to do it the locals' way first. Anyone who believes "I know the right way—the only way—to do business" shouldn't go abroad.

- *Time-change tolerance.* The more difficult it is for people to adjust to jet lag and the effects of travel, the less they probably ought to do it. Assigning someone who suffers severe jet lag to an office in Moscow and expecting them to fly back to Toronto every two weeks is almost certainly a horrible idea. Likewise, people who get confused by time-zone differences probably shouldn't be subjected to them. Find people with a facility for these things.

- *Cultural-time flexibility.* People who understand that different cultures think differently about time, and who can adapt themselves to those cultural differences, will do much better overseas than those who don't. A domestic manager with a penchant for strict punctuality at the home office may simply be viewed as quirky (except in Switzerland or Scandinavia). But in Africa or Latin America, that person is likely to be a disaster.

KEYS TO FINDING THE RIGHT PEOPLE: UNDERSTAND WHERE YOU'RE SENDING THEM

So how do you find employees who fit this profile? How do you pick the right person? There are two keys here: *know what you're sending them into,* and *know your people.*

A lot is written about how employees being sent overseas need to research the culture, language, and customs of the place they're being sent to. That's sound advice. How often is it suggested that the *people doing the sending* need to do the same thing? Practically never. But if you look carefully at the list above, it becomes clear that this is absolutely crucial. Choosing people to send overseas can't be done with a one-size-fits-all checklist. Many of the key characteristics we've written about in earlier chapters *depend on context*.

Consider the story we opened the book with—the woman on the plane, flying into a conservative Muslim country. It was clear in thirty seconds that she had been a tremendously poor choice. But what couldn't be seen, even with the front-row seat Bruce had to that incident, was *who had done the choosing*. Did the manager who picked this woman for the assignment know that the target country has strict laws on how women dress? Did he or she know that women are treated very differently from men, both culturally and in business? Given the selection the home office made, it seems likely that they didn't.

Over the years we have seen a long list of preventable disasters because companies did not heed this advice. One company sent an otherwise effective manager—who turned out to be an unrestrained zealot for what he called abortion rights—to a country that was 99 percent Catholic. Another sent a Pakistani-born Pashtun to manage a company in Mumbai, India—while there was little doubt that the man could do the job, this was most unfair to him, because he was resisted and mistrusted in the new country. A third company sent a well-proven woman manager to take on a new factory overseas; her first act was to angrily ban the local language on the factory floor, bringing work to a halt! All of these disasters could have been prevented if the companies had practiced the principles we outline in this book.

So if you are deciding which people to send overseas, you must first *do your homework*. You can't dump all of the responsibility for understanding culture and how it interacts with the people you send on your employees, on your human resources department, or on a "relocation company" that promises smooth transitions no matter what. In fact, any company that makes that promise should probably be avoided—because if you choose the wrong person to send, there's nothing any relocation company can do to make the transition smooth.

What does *do your homework* mean here? Before you even begin trying to find a person to send overseas, you should be able to answer these questions:

- *How does this culture deal with gender, race, and religion?* Do women get treated differently than men? Are some racial or ethnic backgrounds going to run into resistance? How does religion affect the business and legal environment?

- *What's the lay of the land in language?* Is English widely spoken—and if so, *which* English? How much of the local language will your people need? If a foreign language is needed, which dialect?

- *How culturally different is the place?* Is the target country culturally similar to Canada or the United States, such that your people are likely not to find it very different? Has the target society created spaces within which Western cultural norms are acceptable—and if so, can your business be done within those confines? Or is the local culture so different that your people may be tempted to try to change it to suit their own needs?

- *What's the local sense of time?* Are folks in the target country punctual? Do they adhere to a Western sense of the clock as a strict controller of the business day? Or do they view time differently, with less urgency or more flexibility?

KEYS TO FINDING THE RIGHT PEOPLE: KNOW YOUR PEOPLE

Once you have a handle on these things, you're ready to begin thinking about whom to send. But here again, companies tend to rush to judgment, usually because they have a "process" in place for deciding such things. We'll talk more in the next chapter about one of the processes that most commonly creates problems—the "it's my turn" phenomenon.

But the point here is not to write the Ideal Human Resource Process for you. Rather, it's to make a point that too many companies miss: *know your people*. Companies that land in hot water because they sent the wrong person overseas universally wish they had thought of this ahead of time.

How do you suppose the next meeting went between the woman who was deported from the strict Muslim country and the manager who sent her? Or how do you suppose the representative in France was received after his company's sales fell through the floor? Don't you think those managers wished they had known that the woman they were sending had a headstrong feminist streak, or that the man they relied on hated the French language?

Of course they did. So how do you avoid making the same mistake?

This is where the title of this chapter comes into play. Put simply, if you don't already know your employees closely (and some companies, particularly small and successful ones, do), now is the time to find out who they are. This is not an exercise you can conduct by reading résumés. CVs are not going to tell you whether people think everybody in the world speaks English, or if they believe that the American Way is the only way to do business, or that anybody who shows up five minutes late to a meeting is personally insulting them.

GETTING ON THE SAME PAGE

To get at these things—to discover whether one of your people is really suited to an overseas task—you're going to have to talk to them. Not in a pro forma, here's-a-checklist kind of way, but in a real conversation.

There must be two starting points to this conversation. First, both manager and potential expatriate have to trust each other. If either one believes the other is going to try to do him in, they're doomed from the start. This is elementary in business, but it bears repeating. This has to be an honest conversation, and that demands trust.

Second, the touchstone of the entire exercise must be *advancing the interests of the company*. Of course, employees should share in the rewards if the company does well—that's Management 101. But if the point is to choose somebody who will do the best job overseas, then make that the point. Certainly, other interests will be at play—the employee's future career path, the manager's role in ongoing oversight of the person sent overseas. But it's a lot easier to have an honest conversation if everybody's on board with the larger point of the exercise. Think, too, about how great a role *trust* will play once the candidate gets overseas and starts sending back impressions, assessments, and recommendations. If a solid base of trust is in place, the North American–based executive is going to be much more inclined to accept those inputs with respect, even if they strike him as odd or perhaps make him uncomfortable. This will in turn enable the new overseas-based manager to be much more effective for the organization that sent her.

Oftentimes there *is* a larger point—and not simply to add to the company's bottom line. Before he left to form an independent facilitation company, Bruce was asked by his British employer to take over a troubled, complex project in electronics manufacturing. His company had gotten a contract from the government of

Egypt to provide a highly reliable and rugged communications system that would be used to ensure that the phased evacuation of the Sinai Peninsula went smoothly and without the loss of civilian lives. The project was behind schedule, and the company was in trouble.

As government contracts usually do, this one had a deadline and severe penalty clauses if it was not met. It would have been easy to simply cast the problem in terms of the *company's* interests. Most of the time, that's what companies do—talk in terms of their own bottom line.

In this case, the project was far more important than whether the company earned a few million dollars or not. If the system and all of its intricate equipment were not delivered on time and to specifications, with strict quality control, innocent people would die. This is common in war zones, even those with "cease-fires" in effect, and the Sinai was no exception.

So to get the point across and get everybody onto the same page, Bruce started his work at the factory by putting together a slide show. It contained dramatic pictures of unarmed Palestinians and Israeli citizens being strafed and harmed. It contained maps (where the heck is the Sinai, anyway?) and images of people moving undisturbed through crowded markets. He asked every employee in the factory to take a half hour or so to watch it, in groups of about forty (to whom coffee and tea were served).

Everyone did see it that first day. As they walked out of the cafeteria, many had tears in their eyes. From that point forward, *everybody understood what the point was*. The entire factory, from assemblers to engineers to managers, was on the same page. (The wonderful convergence of purpose led to this project being shipped to Egypt at noon on the day that the contract called for delivery—and on the same day as the birth of Bruce and his wife's first child—making it a day very hard to forget!)

Your business may not save lives in war zones. But if you really believe in what you do, we'll bet that that helps people. The widgets you make, the service you provide—if you're doing it right, it's making a positive difference in somebody's life.

So that's the starting point for your honest conversation. It's not about the manager's ego or the employee's ego. It's about what you're trying to accomplish together.

HONEST CONVERSATIONS

Setting that stage is critical because, as we said above, the most important thing is to *get to know the people you're thinking about sending overseas*. Since you've done your homework, you have some idea of what you're sending them into. If you're really lucky, you may have been there yourself and have firsthand knowledge. Now you need to find out if your potential expatriate has what it takes to go there and get the job done. To find that out, you're going to have to talk candidly about the things we've discussed in the previous four chapters.

This begins with an honest talk about race, gender, family, and attitudes toward them. HR departments may shiver and say, "You can't ask *that*!" and no doubt such issues are sensitive enough to warrant legal consultation in order to establish appropriate guidelines. However, laws proscribing the asking of certain questions generally apply to candidates interviewing for a job with your organization. But once someone is an employee of your firm, the restrictions are far fewer. Your human resources department chief can guide you in this. As a rule of thumb, practices based on *respect* will generally pass most legal tests.

This is a tricky thing, because we've long since lost the knack for talking about these things with honesty and candor. The old saw "Never discuss religion or politics" infects the office as much as the family table. But you as manager need to be open about the requirements of the job—what the cultural constraints are on the other side—and ask for an honest answer on whether the employee is up to the task. If he is known to be open with his religious beliefs, can he operate in an environment where that may get him in serious trouble? If she has built her career on breaking glass ceilings, can she deal with a culture where theirs aren't ready to be broken just yet? These may be awkward topics, but far better that you talk about them now then after the company has lost $750,000 on an unsuccessful assignment.

Language aptitude is easier to test for, or so we think. Years ago, Bruce interviewed for a senior marketing position with a company in upstate New York. They wanted to test his Spanish because the position would require travel to Colombia and working with partners and personnel there. The local managers in New York, however, didn't speak Spanish, so they found a Cuban assembler in the factory and brought him into the room to ask questions. Every time he spoke, Bruce had to ask him three times to repeat himself. Have you ever heard Cuban Spanish? They drop all endings and speak at sixty-nine words a second. Based on this "interview," the HR head in Rochester (who had obviously *not* done her homework, since she assumed that all Spanish is the same) said that Bruce was no good. But the posting was to South America, where Spanish is spoken much more slowly—more like Andy Griffith's English. So if you're testing for language *ability*, make sure it's a realistic test for the actual conditions of the job.

Make sure that the conversation also covers attitudes about language. If somebody has taken the time to learn *a* language voluntarily (forgotten high school French may not count!), he or she is probably willing to do it again. Somebody who reacts badly to the idea—many Americans are more afraid of learning a foreign language than they are of learning math!—probably won't make even the most basic effort needed. We like to laugh at stories like the one in the cell-phone commercial where the businessman overseas mangles a Chinese phrase (because he didn't get a cell-phone connection, of course) and badly insults his Chinese host, who immediately storms off. But in fact, that *does* happen, usually when people aren't serious about trying to learn enough of the language to be polite. Don't let it happen to you.

Talking about trying to change the world is like talking about religion—we stay away from both topics, usually because we're afraid that we'll run into a missionary who will try to convert *us*! This is where being on the same page about the mission of the company helps. It gives you a starting point you can both agree on and opens the door to the bigger conversation, which is *how are we trying to help people over there?* As we explained back in chapter 5, that has to be through the business and the business only. Any hints that somebody is a "meddler"—that he is likely to shoot off on tangents, to "save the locals from themselves"—have to be spotted now. Make sure you understand as much as you can about your employee's motives in wanting to be sent overseas, and make sure that "rescuing the poor, benighted natives" is not one of them.

As we saw previously, this extends to family members as well. This is an even stickier area, but it has to be tackled head-on. If the job calls for a lengthy relocation, you're not just sending your employee, you're sending his entire family, and what they do in that country will reflect on your company, whether they work for you or not. So you need to understand *their* motives as well. Are they likely to meddle in the affairs of the locals or to react badly to differences? Are they likely to rub people from another culture the wrong way, perhaps by spurning their ideas or their language? Would you feel comfortable having the spouse, or the kids, represent your company at a public function? If the answer is no, think twice, because that may not be a hypothetical question at all.

Finally, it is important to understand your prospective expatriate's sense of time. Are schedules and being on time important to her? Does he get confused in translating times across time zones? Is she strongly affected by travel from one time zone to another?

If any of these are mission critical for a particular job, then you've got to get somebody with the right qualities.

SUMMARY

We've spent the first part of this book introducing the things it takes for the people you send overseas to be successful in international business. As we've repeatedly argued, there's no magic formula, no singular checklist, and no way you can give your employees an aptitude test or scan their résumés for the answers. In the international arena, context is everything: where are you sending people, for how long, to do what? The world is complicated, and people are complicated; we shouldn't expect easy models to capture all of that.

What that leaves us with is both simple and complex: *know what you're asking your people to do*, and *know your people*. You have to apply these to your company and your circumstances, but you've got to take these steps to be sure you're sending the right people:

- Know the characteristics for international success—what we've laid out in the early chapters of this book.
- Understand where you're sending your people and what kinds of demands the unfamiliar culture is likely to place on them. You can't know you've got the right person unless you can answer the question "Right person for *what*?"
- Make sure that you and your people are on the same page. Do you share the same goals for the company? If goals aren't shared, failure is a lot more likely.
- Have an honest conversation with the person you're considering sending. Talk through the requirements of the job, what you're hoping the assignment will achieve, and what talents and characteristics it will take to accomplish that. Get

to know your prospective assignee as a person, not as a human resources file.

We recognize that this is an unusual way of doing business, especially for large organizations with complex structures, defined personnel policies, and often-rigid hierarchies. But all the organizational rules in the world don't obviate the realities of the international realm, or the requirements of success in it. If you're serious about helping your company, you've got to adapt to those realities, just as the people you send will have to do.

8

But It's My Turn!

UP TO THIS POINT, we've given you a sense of how to go about picking the right people to send overseas. Much of what we've written about isn't new—scores of academic studies, mostly buried in textbooks and scholarly journals, make some of these same points. The literature on selecting people to send overseas who will be successful goes back thirty-five years or more. So why do we need to keep repeating it? Why are we writing this book?

There are several reasons, and which one fits you will vary. For some companies, it's difficult to filter the research into terms that are useful in practice. If that's the case, we hope this book helps you. But far too many other companies fall into one of two categories: they either choose employees for the *wrong* reasons, or they pick people for *no reason at all*.

ANY VOLUNTEERS?

If the latter sounds unrealistically harsh, consider this. About five years ago, Bill met an engineer who was working for a medium-size precision-manufacturing firm in Indiana. Like a lot of companies in the early part of the decade, this one had decided that it needed to develop international connections—especially (as was all the rage at the time) in China. For several years, the "China price" concept drove decisions across a lot of economic sectors, and this company was very much caught up in that movement.

Unfortunately, the company had always been almost exclusively domestic, with most of its suppliers and customers located around the American Midwest—the so-called rust belt. From the engineering staff up to the CEO's office, no one had any expertise in China, or in international in general. But they *knew* they had to get in the game.

Their first move, therefore, was to identify potential partners in China—mostly through thirdhand contacts, networking through their domestic partners until they got to someone who had done some deal or another with a Chinese firm. They figured, well, it's a start, and hoped that these initial contacts would lead to others—not an unreasonable hope in a business world driven by network connections.

They then faced a problem: whom do we send to pursue these contacts? With no obvious Chinese expertise on hand, they did what far too many companies do: asked for volunteers and picked the first person to raise his hand. This turned out to be the man Bill met, who had had a good career as an engineer and a designer, but no international experience—had, in fact, never been outside North America. Yet the company bought him a plane ticket, gave him the list of targets and a budget for translators, and said, "Off you go—good luck!"

Needless to say, he came back empty-handed some weeks

later. He'd learned a fair amount about Chinese culture and ways of doing business, if only because he was starting from zero. Within a year, he had taken that knowledge with him to a new firm that was already global and better able to make good decisions about international deployments.

As surprising as this story is, it's not uncommon. Across several surveys, 40 to 50 percent of companies that send people overseas admit to having no formal process to decide who goes. Many companies just haven't thought this through. If this is *your* company, we hope this book can help.

THE ROAD TO THE CORNER OFFICE RUNS THROUGH BEIJING

One alternative to sending people based on no criteria is sending them for the wrong ones. Since "globalization" burst on the North American business scene in the 1980s and 1990s, dozens, if not hundreds, of articles have discussed the importance of developing "globally competent managers." In recent years, major publications have been proclaiming overseas experience to be "essential" to managerial development, even claiming that going overseas is "the single most powerful means of enhancing one's career." Increasingly, companies with international operations—as many as 50 percent of them—have taken to intentionally building international experiences into the career paths that lead to their senior executive positions.

This approach has two dangers—for the company and for employees. From the company perspective, it amounts to taking your eye off the ball. The primary purpose of sending somebody overseas to do business is to *do business*. Even though most companies (more than 85 percent, by some studies) don't calculate the return on the investment of sending someone overseas, that return *does* exist and *can* be calculated. As we've pointed out repeatedly, failure is expensive—from direct costs to reputational damage to lost opportunities to damaged careers and lives.

Sending people overseas because they need international exposure—especially if you're not simultaneously making sure they have the capabilities for the assignment—is a sure way to increase your failure rate. If you put in place a system for comparing those capabilities with the needs of the task—as we've been advising throughout the first half of this book—and then override that system in the interest of broader career-development goals, you have largely wasted your time and money. You've also been unfair to the company.

Another danger is that you will skew the incentive system for your employees. A lot of ink is spilled about how to get people to accept overseas assignments—not an easy task, given the logistical and psychological obstacles to relocating to another country, especially with a family in tow (or left behind). Companies and HR consultants have spent years fine-tuning compensation packages and reentry systems so that people will say yes despite those obstacles. Given the resistance, it's small wonder that companies have often been eager to send the willing rather than the capable.

But if you adopt a system that requires people who have higher ambitions to spend time abroad, you are also altering the incentive structure—and probably not the way you wanted to. You will certainly attract more people to your international assignments, but for all the wrong reasons. Under the old "Who wants to go?" system, you might hope that the people volunteering to accept expatriate postings might by chance also have some of the characteristics—flexibility, adaptability, language skill and willingness, cross-cultural comfort—that are necessary to succeed.

But under a road-to-the-corner-office system, you will attract people with qualities—primarily, ambition—completely divorced from those characteristics of success in the international arena. Worse, you will have people who, *because* of ambition, are willing to do whatever it takes—including presenting themselves as more flexible or adaptable or culturally diplomatic than they really are—to get where they want to go.

This opens up another danger: relying too heavily on information that is self-reported. Some international relocation consultancies have "assessment tools" or "qualification inventories" that purport to measure the qualities needed for success overseas. These present an attractive solution to the challenges we raised in our initial chapters: how do you avoid sending people who are going to crash and burn?

The problem, though, is that these "inventories" rely almost exclusively on answers given *by the employee*. The more "acceptable" answer (generally on an "agree/disagree" scale) is often easy for people to spot. If you tell your managers that they need to get an overseas assignment if they want to advance and then ask them, "Do you feel an obligation to share your religious beliefs with others?" do you really think they're going to say *yes*?

This points back to a conclusion in the previous chapter: there is no escape from the need to really know your people, *as people*. If you're relying on scores and graphs on a piece of paper—dubious metrics compiled from self-reported answers to transparent questions—you're almost begging people to manipulate the system, especially if you have skewed the incentives so that people think they "have" to go overseas to get ahead in their careers.

BUT SHE DID SO WELL IN DUBUQUE . . .

Many businesses will avoid these mistakes—they will think about whom to send (rather than picking randomly), and they will think about sending people based on the job at hand. But those that avoid these traps will often fall into another: selecting people solely on the basis of technical ability in the field. Domestically, this often makes some sense: if somebody did a good job of turning around your factory in Peoria, they can reasonably be expected to do the same thing in Kokomo. But as we've seen in previous chapters, this logic goes out the window when you start crossing international boundaries.

Bruce witnessed a tragic example of this point a few years ago, when a major American telecommunications company took one of its star performers in the domestic market and decided he would therefore be a star in Bulgaria—a country that had just months before emerged from dark decades under the hammer and sickle of the Soviet Union and that had not yet figured out how free markets work. The man was friendly enough (most Americans are), but he violated every rule of Bulgarian culture and protocol in *demanding* a meeting with the newly appointed minister of communications. Of course he was also bitterly upset that the minister spoke no English, in a country that had been kept securely behind the Iron Curtain for many years, serving the massive Soviet Union. He compounded his many faux pas by using U.S. telecommunications jargon and technical terms that the besieged interpreter was at a loss to even begin to translate into Bulgarian.

Bruce was called in to help and quickly saw the seriousness of the problem. When he sat down with the American in a private meeting in a Sofia restaurant, he was not surprised to hear the American executive splutter, "Well, it's high time these people woke up and did things the right way!" Not only is the "right" way rarely the American way in other countries, but this executive genuinely believed that he could simply gather all the practices that had accounted for his successes in the USA and just drop them into a new country as if they were spare parts. He also found it inconceivable that the Bulgarian telecom system bequeathed to them by the Soviets was mostly a mess of antiquated copper wire, and that the Bulgarians were either a decade away from getting things updated or would be compelled like many other redeveloping countries to make the "copper leap" and emphasize primarily wireless and cellular communications. The executive was finally recalled to the States, but not until souring the market for other Western companies, too, for some months. The problem wasn't resolved until a few of those companies demonstrated more mature wisdom and sent the right people for the right reasons to Bulgaria.

OFF TO THE GULAG WITH YOU!

Now another dark point. Despite the hoopla about globalization being the wave of the future, too many businesses still use international postings as punishments, or, arguably worse, as ways of solving personnel problems at home. "Fred's been a pain here at the home office," they might say. "Let's ship him overseas to Bangkok, where he can't do as much damage." This is particularly a danger for companies that have international operations but do not *think globally*—that is, they do some business overseas, but see it as peripheral to their "main" market here at home. In those circumstances, an overseas posting to a faraway corner may be seen as not having a significant impact on the bottom line.

A U.S. equipment manufacturer ran into this problem some years back. For over a decade, executives at headquarters decided that they would send their "second string" people to manage their German operations, preferring to keep the best managers at home. Because the overseas assignees were known to be weak leaders, every decision had to be overseen by headquarters, which caused morale problems at all levels, frustration in the home office, and confusion and discontent on the part of the company's German partners. The result was over US$100 million in losses over ten years. Can your company afford this, especially in the days of a harsh economy?

Despite the prolific use of sports terms in business today, international business should not be viewed as a game. Done properly, this serious undertaking embraces respect, patience, and hard thinking. Resist falling for simplistic and flippant references to "rights," too. No employee, at any level, has a *right* to be sent overseas. We urge you rather to use the sound counsel we offer throughout this book (which is recapitulated at the end) in deciding whom should be sent overseas. If you do, you'll enjoy the profits on several levels.

SUMMARY

Having spent the first half of the book talking about how to select people to send overseas, it's important to remind ourselves that a lot of companies and organizations not only don't follow this advice, but pick people for overseas assignments for all the *wrong* reasons. If this is the case at your company, you have to fix these problems before you can even begin to profit from the rest of our advice. If you really want to strive for success with the people you send overseas, make sure you aren't guilty of the sins we've described here:

- Don't send the first person who volunteers. This is particularly true if you're just starting out. The adage "You never get a second chance to make a first impression" applies in spades in the international realm.
- Don't make international experience necessary for advancement in your structure. This simply guarantees that people who aren't any good at it, but who want to move up, will find a way to trick you into sending them anyway.
- Don't use past success in the domestic market as an indicator of likely success overseas! Clearly, the people you send have to know the field. But there is little to no relationship between being a subject expert on your home turf and being effective internationally.
- Don't send people overseas to punish them or to solve your problems at home. If you're going to have a global business,

think globally. This means treating your overseas operations as integral to your business, not as holding pens or peripheral realms for pawning off your domestic difficulties.

No matter what stage of internationalization your company is in now, take a good look at your current practices. Do any of these describe what you're doing? If so, fix it—preferably before you make another overseas assignment.

9

In the Imperial Orbit

HUGO CHÁVEZ WAS ELECTED president of Venezuela in 1998. A populist with pronounced leftist leanings, he immediately began alienating the United States, attacking U.S. foreign policy in Latin America, and making high-profile visits to anti-American leaders, including Fidel Castro (and, before his ouster in 2003, Saddam Hussein). Chávez also signed deals with Iran, North Korea, and Syria. In a major speech to the United Nations in September 2006, Chávez referred to President George W. Bush as "the devil" and the "spokesperson for imperialism," and he was overwhelmingly reelected by Venezuelans a few months later. For its part, the Bush administration returned this rhetoric in kind, accusing Chávez of "praising terrorists" and fomenting war in Latin America.

Despite terrible diplomatic relations, the United States and Venezuela have continued to enjoy strong economic and business ties. The United States accounts for over 20 percent of Venezuela's imports and is the market for over 60 percent of its exports. In return, Venezuela is America's third-largest trading partner in Latin America, and one of the top four foreign suppliers of oil to the U.S. economy. Despite the political rhetoric, business has continued.

But that separation between business and politics has been more wishful thinking than real. In September 2008, Chávez expelled the U.S. ambassador to Venezuela, accusing him of fomenting a coup against his regime. He then recalled his own ambassador to the United States. This set off another round of angry accusations and counteraccusations, which has become somewhat standard fare over the years. A month after the spat over diplomats, Venezuela's government tax agency suddenly declared that the vast majority of McDonald's branches in the country—some 115 restaurants in all—would be closed for investigations into their books for "tax irregularities." This was not the first time Chávez's government had used its authority to go after prominent U.S. companies, shutting down the local offices of Pepsi-Cola and nationalizing the Venezuelan operations of Exxon Mobil and other U.S. oil firms.

Many decried these moves as hurting Venezuelan interests—given the trade interdependence between the two countries—or as just plain crazy. But the businesses affected found out the hard way that sometimes political calculation trumps economic reason, usually with dangerous consequences for the company caught in the cross fire—in this instance, McDonald's lost millions in forgone sales.

The vast majority of textbooks on international business and management are silent on the subject of politics, feeding the assumption that business operates in a separate realm. Likewise, most international business programs at colleges and universities in the United States are thin on the subject of foreign affairs. Most MBA programs have, at best, an elective course that focuses on politics, and some prominent programs don't even have that.

Business education and political education might as well exist on different planets.

But as the Venezuela example indicates, this is a deadly mistake—*especially* for American companies. Here, for the benefit of our Canadian readers, we must make a distinction. The United States has held a unique place in the world for the past sixty years—a role that has significant implications for American businesses operating overseas, but not necessarily for Canadian or European firms. The real benefits of this chapter, therefore, are to our American readers who have mistakenly been taught the mindless mantra that "politics and government never mix." In the international arena, nothing could be further from the truth, as we'll show in this chapter.

BUT I'M AN AMERICAN!

American companies must face two realities when they venture outside their home shores. First, Americans and American enterprises tend to assume they enjoy special protection simply because of the passport they carry. This is understandable given that the United States has, since 1945, been the acknowledged center of world power. All of the major international financial rules and institutions (now coming under increasing strain) were drawn up under American auspices, mostly at Bretton Woods, New Hampshire, in 1944. It is no accident that the headquarters of the World Bank and the IMF are on Pennsylvania Avenue, just a block or two from the White House. The U.S. dollar has, until recently, been the world's reserve currency, giving American companies enormous leverage in the marketplace.

Many of these things are changing—which we will discuss further below. But our first point is that all of these together have created a kind of "untouchability complex" among American businesses—which must immediately be abandoned if you want to be successful.

This is true regardless of what kind of business you are in. Some brands—McDonald's and Pepsi, to recall the Venezuelan example above—are so linked to the world's view of America that it is not surprising that they might become targets when things get volatile. But even operations in sectors that are seemingly far from politics or the American image can be affected. In response to a cross-border airstrike into Syria by American forces in Iraq in October 2008, the Syrian government shut down an American school and a cultural center in Damascus. Anti-American sentiment ran so high in the wake of the attack that even mentioning the prospect of doing business with an American company—or an American businessman—was enough to kill a deal.

American businessmen going abroad can also find that the American reputation precedes them. In the 1980s, the CEO of a U.S.-based Fortune 500 company was traveling to Switzerland. While there, he made arrangements to meet with his counterpart at a Swiss company in the same business. Both companies had worldwide reputations, though they occupied different niches of the market. The meeting hadn't been planned in advance, and no specific proposals were on the table.

Upon his arrival in the Swiss chairman's office, the American was greeted rather coldly. The first words from his frowning Swiss counterpart were "My company is not for sale, sir!"

The American smiled broadly and replied, "That's okay. Mine isn't, either!"

The two then had an excellent two-hour chat about the state of the industry. But that was only possible once the American had skillfully overcome the natural fear of foreign businesses toward American merger-and-acquisition (M&A) tendencies, a fear founded on years of American companies acting in another dimension of the untouchability complex.

ALL POLITICS IS LOCAL—BUT TROUBLE TRAVELS

Companies can also find themselves in trouble depending on *where* they locate their operations—and how much of a price they're willing to pay to be there. They can also run afoul of international politics and U.S. law.

In the mid-1990s, a U.S.-based mining company wanted to establish a start-up mine in the Philippines. The island where the mine was located, unfortunately, was in the heart of contested territory, controlled by a rebel organization with a history of both violent armed resistance and anti-American tendencies. According to charges leveled years later by a whistle-blower, the company tried to finesse the local politics by simply buying the rebels off. This was allegedly done with money, weapons, and access to medical care and "safe areas" where government authorities would not look for rebel leaders.

Although the charges were never adversely resolved, the company suffered twice for having gotten entangled in an area fraught with violent conflict. First, it was publicly blamed when the rebel group captured and killed Americans in the area, seriously damaging its reputation and standing. And it faced a Justice Department investigation of its business practices. The story was widely reported, and the company was eventually bought out.

In another example, a U.S. mining company operated a coal mine in northern Colombia. In early 2001, three leaders of a local coal-miners' union were gunned down, allegedly by right-wing paramilitary groups. A year after the murders, a coalition of families, labor rights activists, and union supporters filed suit against the company in U.S. court, fueled by their perception that the company was in league with the paramilitaries to suppress local workers. The case eventually led to investigations by the government of the Netherlands as well, on behalf of Dutch businessmen who alleged that their claim had been usurped by the American company. Five years later the company was exonerated by the federal district court, but an appeal kept the case going—forcing the company to continue defending itself, costing a great deal of money and more goodwill.

One of our clients in 1992–93 was a private, financially successful American insurance firm. At their request we took them into a newly freed Eastern European country and got their new subsidiary properly licensed, registered, structured, and launched—the first private insurance company in that country in half a century. Everything began well. We advised them on staffing, on government relations, and on the culture in general. And they listened.

But then the head of the company at the time succumbed to that dangerous myth that Americans are the best at everything. He began to hire people he didn't know. Against our written warnings, he even hired former KGB officials who were deeply resented and reviled by the local populace, as well as by the new government. Within a few months the company was in deep trouble: sales had dropped off dramatically, and formal charges were brought against the firm in the host country. The company argued that the host government should be grateful for their presence and should exempt them from prosecution. We probably don't have to tell you how well *that* went down with the local government! Once again: neither Americans nor Canadians have any special rights in the international arena. None.

YOUR REPUTATION PRECEDES YOU— WHETHER YOU KNOW IT OR NOT

The first lesson of international politics for the American businessman is that being American doesn't give you any special privileges overseas. The second is that being American *does* mean that other people look at you differently. Part of this is culture—the image of the "ugly American" still travels far and wide, aided and abetted by American businesses from time to time.

Some of this comes from ignorance. Some years ago, a group of American business students took part in a seminar with Japanese workers. The idea was to get the Americans working on joint projects with their Japanese counterparts, so they could learn how to work in multicultural teams. After a few days of working together, one of the Japanese workers approached the leader of the project and asked, "What does it mean when an American pats you on the back?"

"That you've done a good job" was the answer. "And what does it mean if a Japanese manager pats you on the back?"

"That you've done a bad job," the Japanese worker replied. In their ignorance, the American students had been insulting their Japanese colleagues for days, while learning to get along in multicultural teams! It pays to do your homework before you go abroad!

But while these cultural faux pas stories are common, they miss a more important perception that people overseas often attach to Americans: that American businesses are extensions of U.S. government policy.

This seems laughably silly to American managers, most of whom have never met a U.S. policymaker and have never had any dealings with the U.S. government beyond the IRS or perhaps the Labor Department. But we kid ourselves if we don't realize that relations between American companies and the U.S. government are complex.

Americans tend to view corruption as a foreign practice—hence the existence of the *Foreign* Corrupt Practices Act, which we'll talk about in a few chapters. But the rest of the world knows better, because it has seen corrupt relations between the U.S. government and American companies for years. The Iraq War in particular has brought a lot of these to the surface, although the overseas assumption—justified by dozens of studies and exposés—is that they were there all along.

Take the case of Major John Lee Cockerham of the U.S. army. Stationed in Kuwait and overseeing U.S. government procurement contracts for billions of dollars of supplies, Cockerham was accused in 2007 of taking and hiding nearly US$10 million in bribes from U.S. companies that wanted to sell those supplies to the army. His case alone called into question the validity of some US$6 billion worth of U.S. contracts—and few, especially in the international business community, believed that he was the single bad apple in the barrel.

Sometimes the U.S. government makes no secret of its desire to use American companies to advance an American agenda overseas. In 2007, Google, Yahoo!, and other American Internet companies got into trouble with the U.S. Congress over their business arrangements with the Chinese government. Internet search-engine companies had, as a cost of doing business in China, been turning over individual user data and e-mails to Chinese authorities, particularly on suspect individuals and anybody who searched for information deemed by the government to be politically sensitive or dangerous. According to a subsequent investigation, this practice had led to the arrest, torture, and detention of at least four Chinese citizens.

Members of Congress were outraged and called the general counsels and senior executives of these companies before the House Foreign Affairs Committee for questioning. The message was fairly clear: you are undermining U.S. policy in China, which called for supporting democratization through "peaceful evolution" and "constructive commercial engagement." The U.S. government, in other words, assumed that these companies would act in accordance with U.S. policy and publicly embarrassed and harangued them when they did not. This message was not missed by the rest of the world.

In some instances, the issues raised by a particular business deal can kill it because of the intersection between business and international politics—even when the deal is between close allies. In 2008, the Canadian government forbade the sale of the space operations of a major Canadian company to an American firm. The American firm had significant ties to the U.S. government—as most companies in the U.S. aerospace industry do—which fueled the perception that the sale was primarily political, not business-related. The issues were Canadian sovereignty and national interests—the deal included control of a unique satellite with particular capabilities for surveying the geography of the Arctic. Canada regards the Arctic as an area of special concern and was not keen to allow its more powerful neighbor to the south control over an important asset, especially one that might be used against it.

Interestingly, the proposed sale was itself prompted by U.S. national security laws—in particular, laws that limited foreigners' access to work on "sensitive areas," such as satellites for U.S. customers. This left the Canadian company with a very limited customer base, since it could not sell its services *as a Canadian company* to U.S. clients. Politics had at once made the sale both necessary and impossible.

In another incident in 2001, the U.S. government wished to target Somalia's only two Internet-service-provider firms, claiming that they were supporting al-Qaeda. One of the companies relied on an international network gateway that was jointly run by AT&T and British Telecom. This gave the U.S. government a source of leverage, but also contributed to the perception that Western corporations sometimes merely act as arms of American foreign policy.

THE CAT'S-PAW REPUTATION

The clear danger is that American businesses will be suspected of being cat's-paws of the U.S. government. This fear has been compounded in recent years because some companies *are* agents of U.S. policy abroad. Some of this is blatantly obvious: the increasing privatization of U.S. military functions has turned some companies, such as Halliburton and its former subsidiary KBR, into well-paid bearers of U.S. policy, sometimes even the primary conductors of it. In much of the world historical memories are long, and people can easily recall companies that were closely entangled in—or, sometimes, even driving—major U.S. foreign-policy initiatives.

In 1951, Jacobo Arbenz Guzmán was elected president of Guatemala in a wave of mass populism, fueled by farm laborers and the poor. At the time, the United Fruit Company, an American corporation, owned all of Guatemala's banana production and export, as well as the country's telephone and telegraph systems, and most of its railroads. After several years of land reform pressures that threatened to break UFC's monopolies, the U.S. government intervened in 1954, organizing and equipping a coup that toppled the Arbenz regime and brought a new government to power under Castillo Armas, who was much more protective of both U.S. anticommunist interests as well as United Fruit economic concerns.

In the intervention, it was not lost on Latin America and much of the rest of the world that the ties between United Fruit and the U.S. government were extremely close. President Eisenhower's personal secretary was married to the head of United Fruit's public relations department. The assistant secretary of state for Inter-American Affairs, John Moors Cabot, was the brother of a former United Fruit CEO. Both Secretary of State John Foster Dulles, and his brother, the director of the CIA, Allen Dulles, were involved with United Fruit through their law firms, which had done extensive work in setting up the company's holdings in Guatemala in the first place. To many in Latin America, it wasn't clear whether this was a U.S. company cooperating with American policy, or American policy being shaped to benefit a U.S. company. What *was* clear was that Latin American antipathy toward the United States grew radically from this intervention.

While many Americans regard this as ancient history, there is a long line of connections between American businessmen and powerful positions in the U.S. government. Robert McNamara was the first person outside the Ford family to head the Ford Motor Company, another American corporate icon. He went on to become secretary of defense under Presidents Kennedy and Johnson, then took over the World Bank in 1968, completing the cycle of corporation, U.S.-government-agency, and international-financial-institution jobs.

McNamara is hardly alone. James Schlesinger, who served as director of the CIA, secretary of defense, and secretary of energy, was also a senior adviser to Lehman Brothers. Donald Rumsfeld, who was U.S. ambassador to NATO and served twice as secretary of defense, also worked as CEO of G. D. Searle, the pharmaceutical giant, and General Instrument Corporation. Caspar Weinberger, Ronald Reagan's secretary of defense for most of his two terms, was vice president and general counsel for the Bechtel Group of companies, a powerful industrial consortium. George Shultz, Reagan's secretary of state, was president of Bechtel. William Perry, one of Clinton's secretaries of defense, was director of the Electronic Defense Laboratories of Sylvania, and later president of ESL, an electronics firm.

Some authors have written books telling stories of the connections between politics and business in America. Some, such as Ben Wattenberg's *The Wealth Weapon*, have been around for decades. Others, such as John Perkins's *Confessions of an Economic Hit Man*, which made it to the *New York Times* bestseller list, are more recent. But stories of American business involvement in politics have been around for some time.

In light of this history, it is small wonder that much of the rest of the world saw government-corporate collusion when Richard B. Cheney, former CEO of Halliburton, became vice president of the United States. But the belief that the political and business worlds are inseparable also arises because, in much of the rest of

the world, they are inseparable—and this is commonly understood. The Chinese army, the government branch bearing the
main burden of China's defense policy, owns a wide array of businesses: electronics and aerospace firms, pharmaceutical manufacturers, vegetable growers, even an airline. Although China is a
particularly stark example, in most of the world, most of the time,
the powerful—in business and in politics—tend to be intertwined.

What does this mean for American businessmen? It means
that, although we tend to assume that there is a divide between the
public and private sectors in America, others around the world
are unlikely to see it that way. If your company does any business
with the U.S. government—almost regardless of what kind of
business it is—some will suspect you of being, in essence, an arm
of U.S. government policy. Some may even suspect that your operation is a "front" for other interests—such stories are much
more commonly believed outside the United States than in it, especially across the developing world.

These suspicions can occur even if your company has nothing to do with the U.S. government, and they can be very difficult
to dispel. Dealing with them requires an extra measure of
transparency—not to put yourself at an obvious commercial disadvantage, of course, but to be as open and transparent as you can
about your business dealings, to give your potential partners as
much comfort as you can that you are *not*, in fact, a shill for Washington.

When Bruce was serving as a senior international manager for
a British company, he was assigned to negotiate a multimillion-
dollar transaction with a large German firm. Although civility
reigned in the meetings, days went by with no progress. Finally he
asked one of the senior German players the real reason for the
stalemate, for it surely was not about price. Imagine his surprise
when the German executive replied that they were concerned that
the British company was in fact doing business in a country that
was at that time strongly inimical to German interests. Although it

took some serious persuasion back in the UK, Bruce was finally able to obtain a list of the company's clients in the country of concern, proving at once that the German fears were unfounded. This transparency not only had instant good effects for all, it taught us then and there the unsurpassable value of transparency in international business.

POLITICS AND BUSINESS *DO* MIX– BUT NOT ALWAYS WELL

This has implications at the individual level as well when you send your people overseas to negotiate on your behalf. We talked a few chapters ago about some of the more obvious personal characteristics—gender, race, religion—and how they can affect employees' effectiveness. Given worldwide perceptions about the intertwining of politics and business, we need to add *political proclivities* to that list. Not that it matters what party your employees identify with, or whom they voted for in the last election. But politics, like religion, is difficult to talk about among strangers. Employees who have strong beliefs about America's role in the world, the history of its foreign policy, or its position on important international political issues need to either learn to hide those beliefs or not go abroad. We're very serious about this.

In one of his executive positions with a major American multinational, Bruce was assigned to travel with another American executive of the company who had had little exposure to the international marketplace. Although the other executive was a likable fellow, Bruce cautioned him on the long flight over to the Middle Eastern country that he should avoid all comments on local politics and especially on U.S. foreign policy. Bruce had also advised that any demo videotapes be sent over via international courier weeks in advance because such tapes were highly suspect to the customs officials of the country they were flying to.

Unfortunately, that advice was ignored. As soon as they arrived, customs officials, in a routine baggage inspection, seized the tapes angrily and declared them to be "American-Zionist propaganda." Of course they were no such thing, but an unpleasant two-hour delay at the airport followed while officials got around to viewing the tapes on a special monitor they had set up in a small office somewhere far from where Bruce and his colleague were detained. Hoping there would be no more incidents, they proceeded to their hotel, where they were warmly met by officials from the host government—the clients.

An hour or so into the dinner, Bruce's colleague spluttered his resentment over being "treated like some terrorist" by the host government's customs authorities. A quiet chill settled over the table, even after the host explained civilly that videotapes really ought not be brought into the country in one's baggage. But not half an hour later, the executive made an offhand remark about how U.S. policy was shaped to "remind the Arabs of their place in the Middle East." Do we even have to say that the deal was killed in that instant, and that the host delegation left the table in silence and canceled the next day's meetings without comment? At all times, and in all countries, leave your political beliefs at home and focus on the mission at hand.

Ironically enough, politics have even been causing American businessmen to have difficulties with their *own* government. Post-9/11, the U.S. government passed sweeping new international banking regulations with the intention of limiting the ability of terrorists to move money into and out of the United States. These were on top of laws that already placed significant restrictions on what kind of overseas bank accounts Americans could hold. Under the new rules, domestic U.S. banks no longer wanted to take the risk of hosting an account whose holder had an address outside the United States—even if that account holder was a U.S. citizen working for a U.S. company or institution.

This has put American expat workers in a serious bind. Their own government has been increasingly aggressive about pressuring foreign banks to shut down bank accounts held by American citizens, regardless of whether they live overseas or not. But American domestic banks have been refusing to take deposits from those same individuals without a U.S. address. National security politics play havoc with international business, down to the lowest levels— and while these obstacles are not insurmountable, management and employees need to be aware of these problems and figure out solutions ahead of time.

THE TIMES, THEY ARE A-CHANGIN'

Finally, we noted above that American business has operated for the last fifty years in a system of American domination of the international financial and economic world. That domination is ending even as we are writing this book. Indeed, we expect that the severe recession into which the U.S. economy is falling at the end of 2008 will be a prime reason why you may be looking to take your company overseas, or expand your international operations. If so, you're very prudent.

We do not know in detail yet what the new international economic order will look like, or what the rules will be—or even who will write them. But a couple of things appear certain. First, the United States is likely to lose its position as *the* primary mover in international business. This likely means more competition from businesses in other countries for the same international market spaces. But if it helps American companies shed their previously strong sense of exceptionalism, that will be a significant benefit.

Second, it seems likely that other parts of the world may recover before the United States does from the present troubles. This seems counterintuitive; many believe that because the United States has been the epicenter of the present economic meltdown, America will also lead the way out. But in reality, many companies around the world are finding that they need to abandon too much dependence on the American market and are beginning to look elsewhere as well. In the short run, this means, again, more competition.

But in the long run, if the United States becomes a more "normal player" on the world business stage—one among a group of important players, instead of the single dominating force—some of the political problems that businesses have run into for decades, described above, may begin to fall away. Companies from Sweden or Denmark or Germany or the UK or Brazil can compete on their own merits, without a lot of excess baggage based on the country they happen to come from. If American businesses can someday reach a future where they can say the same—and that future may be starting to emerge now—that would be a positive development for your business.

SUMMARY

We've pointed out here that, despite the illusion created by business schools and common practice, business and politics are inextricably intertwined. This is *especially* true in the international realm, where politics are not only thoroughly enmeshed in business (and vice versa), but are also much more complex. One overarching message here is to avoid the assumption that too many Americans and Canadians make: that anybody can understand politics because it's an inherently "democratic" field. In truth, international politics are extremely complicated and often very far from democratic.

Beyond this important reminder, we've also laid out the areas where businesses can get in trouble when they don't understand the connections between business and politics. With apologies to our Canadian readers, this chapter has largely been aimed at American businesses, because the United States has occupied a unique place in the world, especially in the "era of globalization" in the 1990s and into the twenty-first century, but also going back to 1945. Most of the environment that international business plays out in was written and structured by Americans, in service of what they thought American interests were. That matters, in various ways—including some that can trip you up when you venture into the international arena as an American business.

When planning your international strategy, make sure you've thought these points through carefully:

- Americans and American businesses do *not* enjoy any special protections overseas simply by being American. In fact, sometimes being an American business can make you a target, especially if you are easily or strongly identified with the United States as a whole.
- Local political issues matter—a lot. By moving your business into a new environment, you automatically become a player in local politics, especially if you're investing in an important or strategic sector of the local economy. Playing by two sets of rules—the locals' political rules, and your home country's—is difficult but necessary.
- Corruption is not just a foreign phenomenon. People in foreign lands are much more ready to believe that Americans are corrupt than we are. Even if you're squeaky-clean, you may have to go to some lengths to prove it.
- Many parts of the world don't share our assumption that the government and the private sector are separate—and sometimes, they're right. Even if you aren't an agent of U.S. policy, others may believe you are, and that affects how they treat you.
- Politics and business *do* mix, but often with very combustible results overseas. Make sure that the people you send to represent your company aren't going to get you in trouble for political views or attitudes.

- The United States has been the center of the world economy for over sixty years—but that isn't set in stone. In fact, it's changing before our eyes. Your broader international strategy has to take this into account. If you build your strategy on an assumption of continued American dominance, you're likely to be disappointed.

We're suggesting *don't neglect to think through the politics of what you're doing*. Domestically, this is often self-evident, but going overseas introduces a lot of new complications. As with other areas we've talked about in this book, if you don't have the in-house expertise to manage these things, *find the help you need*. You can get that help from us, or from any of a number of seasoned professional firms out there who can help you navigate the tricky waters of international politics. But make sure you get the advice you need because this arena, even if you do everything else right, can sink your overseas business.

10

Who Can You Trust?

IN 2008, A MAJOR American private equity firm wanted to do what many companies were doing at the time: develop a substantial presence in Asia. The Chinese market in particular was growing by leaps and bounds, and everybody wanted a piece of the action. The equity firm chose to structure its foothold by partnering with a Japanese leasing company that had a Chinese subsidiary, something few Japanese financial firms possessed. Since the Japanese company needed cash, the deal seemed like a win-win for everybody.

The American firm hired a Chinese businessman to be its point man on the China end of the deal. At the time, it seemed like an excellent move: the point man had an established track record and had helped the equity firm on other business in the region.

The deal began to go sour in the summer of 2008 as the partnership developed difficulties in attracting funding—critical to any financial-services business. As the dispute escalated, the Japanese parent company attempted to remove the local Chinese leadership and replace it with personnel from its American partner. As so often happens, the conflict quickly devolved into charges and countercharges, with lawsuits being filed and threatened. At one point, when the newly appointed management showed up to take possession of the China office, they were chased off by Chinese police, who had been called by the previous management team!

In the course of the conflict, it was alleged that the highly touted point man had engaged in improper dealings. In an effort to raise capital, he was accused of skirting Chinese government currency-control rules by using a personally controlled investment vehicle to lend Hong Kong dollars to the Chinese subsidiary in exchange for renminbi (the currency of the People's Republic of China) at a high interest rate. The deal would also spin off a sizable profit if the renminbi appreciated, which was widely expected at the time.

As so often happens, when the deal came unglued, it became impossible to tell whose interests the point man was serving: the American firm's or the local Chinese subsidiary's. Loyalty and trust become critical issues when billions of dollars are at stake.

Business thrives on many things—money, time, ideas, the usual suspects. But the most important of these is *relationships*. (As we asserted in another chapter, *relationship overarches the deal—always*.) Lawyers will tell you that there's no such thing as an airtight contract that can control somebody's behavior with certainty. This is especially true in the international business arena, where what's legal and what's appropriate are often muddled and muddied and usually poorly understood by both sides.

We'll address other complexities of international partnerships in the next chapter—with a special focus on the Foreign Corrupt Practices Act and the many confusing lines that legislation creates. In this chapter, we want to focus on the *human* element.

Although laws are important—particularly for companies that want to keep from running afoul of them—they cannot guarantee that individuals you rely on won't torpedo your business, intentionally or otherwise.

THERE IS NO SUBSTITUTE FOR TRUST

Plenty of dramatic stories show that trust violated by a single individual has brought companies collapsing to earth. In the mid-1990s, Barings PLC was wiped out by a single trader in Singapore who managed to lose US$1.3 billion through foolish trades that he hid from senior management. Around the same time, a major Japanese bank discovered that it had lost US$1.1 billion through the actions of one bond trader in New York, who had hidden the loss for eleven years. So the generic warning about "bad apples" has long been known.

But in the wake of those mid-1990s scandals, much of the response focused on *regulation*. The problem, it was asserted, was that governments didn't play enough of an oversight role, and that their capacity for doing so was weak (never mind that one of those scandals took place under the nose of the U.S. Federal Reserve). But a few learned the opposite lesson—the correct one, in our view—that there is no substitute for trust, good judgment, and good sense.

So our message in this chapter is simple: you've got to find the right overseas partners to work with. This is not pie-in-the-sky optimism that says we should trust everybody and hope for the best. The destruction of Barings was enough to show that some people should *not* be trusted. What this does mean is that you need to have people you *can* trust.

BUSINESS ISN'T A BLIND DATE: GET TO KNOW YOUR PARTNERS

Perhaps the first lesson that needs to be learned is even simpler: *know whom you're working with*. In 2007, a scandal erupted over toothpaste manufactured in China, some of which had become contaminated with diethylene glycol, a dangerous chemical found in antifreeze products. The story broke initially in Panama, where fifty-one people died of poisoning in early 2007 after using the tainted products. Neighboring countries began pulling Chinese-made products from their shelves, but initial reports in the United States were that this was a problem restricted to Central America. That story lasted about a month, until inspections revealed tainted products showing up on shelves in U.S. stores in Puerto Rico and Miami. The FDA immediately released a warning to the public: toss out all Chinese-made toothpaste until further notice.

Much of the finger-pointing was, of course, aimed back at China and the company that had apparently been caught adulterating its products with dangerous (and less costly) chemicals in an effort to increase its profit margins. This story, along with a series of other China-related manufacturing scandals (poisonous chemicals in pet food, toxic lead-based paint on popular children's toys), caused many to reconsider the wholesale rush to Chinese manufacturing seen in recent years.

But the problems didn't stop there for American businesses. In early 2008, the City of Los Angeles filed criminal charges against four executives at two American import companies that had allegedly brought tainted products into the United States and redistributed them to retailers. Around the same time, a company in Nevada was charged for its role in importing tainted pet food that had led to the deaths of over four thousand pets in the United

States. In both cases, executives claimed that they didn't know what was in the products and hadn't intended to hurt anyone.

The vast networks of manufacturers, distributors, importers, wholesalers, and retailers created by global product chains have created systems where the businesses involved—and the people who run those businesses—barely know one another any more. This is regarded as an inevitable consequence of globalization— the search for efficiencies over ever longer distances and increasingly complicated networks. But this "inevitability" argument hides a critical truth: *every one of these connections is made between human beings, representing their companies*. Just because we can no longer easily see the human connections in the global marketplace from a distance doesn't mean they're not there. At every link in the chain, a judgment is made: *do I do business with this person or not?* In the international arena, where enforcement mechanisms are more difficult and cultural differences make understanding more laborious, trust must be made central to this decision. Legal issues aside, each of the businesses caught up in the scandals of tainted products from China had violated this basic business rule: *know who your partners are, and know that you can trust them.*

Sometimes not knowing your partners can lead to trouble not because your partners are duplicitous or criminal, but simply because they're a bad match. In 2003, an American PR firm wanted to build a market presence in Japan. The firm specialized in high-tech communications work, which seemed well suited to the Japanese market, but the high price of Japanese real estate and attendant overhead costs were daunting. The company came up with what it thought was a clever strategy: find a local partner in the same business with whom it could share space and overhead, thus reducing the cost and hopefully providing the potential for growth for the benefit of both companies.

The PR firm managed to find a small Japanese communications company willing to enter into the arrangement, but almost immediately encountered problems. First, because the PR firm was not incorporated in Japan, the Japanese company saw it as a kind of second-class citizen—an aspect of local business culture that the American firm had not understood. Second, and ultimately more damaging, the Japanese company wasn't interested in the sorts of high-tech communications that its American partner was selling—it preferred to focus on its core business, Japanese-English translation services. Ultimately, the American PR firm ended the partnership and started over—in large part because it hadn't taken the time up front to really understand whom they were dealing with, and whether the match was a good one.

The PR firm did, however, learn its lesson. A few years later, when it wanted to move into China, it first found a Chinese executive skilled in communications and brought her to the company's main site in the United States. She worked at the American headquarters for a year and a half, learning the company's culture, mission, and vision for its future. For executives used to thinking of globalization as always meaning "faster," eighteen months can seem like an eternity. But in this case, the strategy paid off: at the end of that time, both the company and its Chinese partner knew each other well enough to know what it would take to make the new venture in China work. A few years later, the China subsidiary had over a dozen employees and was the company's fastest-growing arm.

REVIVING COMMON SENSE: YOU CAN'T FIX IT WITH RULES

We tend, in business as well as in the public arena, to try to substitute rules for real human relationships. We hope that we can find the perfect algorithm that will solve our problems for us and keep us from the risk of making the wrong decisions. Yet trying to write rules ahead of time, to cover every situation, usually creates more problems than it solves. This is particularly true when dealing with overseas assignments and partnerships.

A few years ago the authors heard a story from a business executive whose company had several partners and subsidiaries across Europe. The company was pursuing a broad European strategy for its products, which meant using its subsidiaries and partners to negotiate with multiple European governments at the same time. The executive in charge of the entire effort received a letter one day from one of the company's own people, the man who was spearheading the negotiations in Sweden—a highly respected employee who had an excellent track record with the company. The letter was an invitation to the man's upcoming wedding to a Swedish local in Stockholm. The executive, acting according to predetermined company rules about potential conflicts of interest, immediately removed the man from the negotiations.

Although we never heard the outcome of that case, it isn't hard to imagine the potential spillover costs of such a rigid rule. How much of its investment in this highly successful employee would the company lose by sending him home—and possibly losing him in the near future? What would the effect of this be on other expatriate employees in other countries who might develop relationships with locals? And, most important to our purposes here, what message does such a rule send to your foreign partners? To base a rule strictly on nationality sends a clear signal: we trust nobody who isn't one of us. Imagine such a company's difficulties working with foreign partners in the future.

WHEN YOU'VE GOT THE RIGHT PEOPLE, TRUST THEM

If the first lesson in finding the right people is *know whom you're working with*, the second is *be willing to trust your partners*. Again, this doesn't mean you trust them all blindly. But you are asking for failure if you make it clear—as the company above did with its policy in Sweden—that foreign nationals will never be treated as equals.

Unfortunately, many companies—without thinking about it—don't trust their foreign partners. A few years ago the communications division of a major American technology company decided to expand some of its operations into Argentina. It had had success in the business in several other countries and certainly had the technical expertise. The company spent millions building the business from the ground up, on its own, without any significant local partnerships. But the venture failed to attract customers and eventually had to be spun off. The assumption that "we know what we're doing" often goes hand in hand with the idea that the locals can't be trusted and has led to a great many disasters similar to this one.

Although internal company rules that discriminate against foreign nationals are a bad idea, companies do have to deal with the established rules and laws of other countries. Some of these rules, particularly laws regarding employment, firing, and quitting, can affect the trust between the company and its overseas partner. Your company *must* understand the rules of the environment it's operating in, because what you take as simply a gesture of trust may have unintended consequences.

An American high-tech company decided to expand overseas to Europe and wanted to do so quickly, fearing that not moving fast would put it behind the global competition. Unfortunately, in trying to get the deal done in three months, company executives didn't take the time to understand the labor rules in the Netherlands, their first targeted market. They found a new hire at a local company who they thought would be perfect to help them get up and running. Because he had a lifetime contract with the employer he was leaving, they offered him the same, not understanding that many European countries have no concept of "at will" employment, and a lifetime contract really does mean for life. The company managed the transition reasonably well anyway, and has since learned a great deal about Dutch labor law, but it also has potential liabilities going forward that it will have to deal with carefully.

So understanding your partners is critical, as is being willing to trust them—without being so blind to the larger environment that trust becomes an unintended liability. But how do you go about finding the best partners to work with?

DON'T TRY THIS ALONE

Regrettably, finding the best partners is considered by many seasoned international executives to be the thorniest and most complex element of international business. We count ourselves among those executives. Stated simply, *you're going to need help in this area*. A single chapter in a book cannot possibly give you enough information or guidance because so much is dependent on where in the world you're trying to work, the kind of business you're trying to do, whom you're working with—and such decisions as whether the people ought to be contractors, representatives, distributors, agents, or something else altogether. Our purpose here has simply been to introduce you to these complexities, and to impress upon you the paramount importance of doing this right— by getting advice from seasoned professionals. If you don't get that help from us, then please get it from one of a number of other competent professional service firms out there. Do not tackle this without seasoned counsel. It's just too important. As you can see from the examples in this chapter, it can crash your company unless you tackle it properly.

SUMMARY

We've given you an introduction to the other side of the table. When you send your people overseas, they have to work with other people—partners, agents, distributors, representatives of other companies. Picking those people is even more challenging than making sure you're sending the right people from your side—but just as vital. Our purpose here hasn't been to make you an expert in this area—no book chapter could ever do that—but simply to get you thinking about the key points. You'll be much better served, and your overseas business more successful, if you keep these in mind:

- Business really isn't a blind date—you've got to know whom you're working with. This is not a call for typical "due diligence," which is generally done by documents that can far too easily be faked. This is about really getting to know your partners, person to person.
- Don't try to control relationships with rules that cover all situations. There has to be room for flexibility. Rules can quickly become arbitrary handcuffs.
- When you do identify the right people, be ready to trust them. Partnerships that don't incorporate mutual trust rarely get you where you want to go.
- Finding trustworthy international partners is very difficult and complex. If you don't already have a trusted network you can build on, get help—from our company or another like it. Don't try to do this alone, especially if you're just starting out for the first time.

11

Honest, Officer, I Didn't Think It Was Bribery!

IN LATE 2007, THE U.S. Court of Appeals upheld the conviction of two American executives charged with bribery of foreign officials under the Foreign Corrupt Practices Act (FCPA). While conviction of American businessmen under the FCPA is unlikely to shock anybody, the case illustrated how poorly the legal terrain was understood, and how far the FCPA's reach really extends.

The executives were employed by a U.S.-based, publicly traded company whose business was food exports to Third World nations. In the last of the 1990s and into the early part of the next decade, the two executives were found to have paid money to officials of a particularly poor Third World nation in exchange for a lowering of taxes and duties on the food they were importing into the country. For most of us, this seems pretty cut-and-dried: they bribed foreign officials, they were caught, they were convicted. But the road from bribe to conviction was not straight.

The executives' attorneys argued that the payments did not

fall under the FCPA because they did not qualify as what the FCPA calls a "business nexus"—that is, payments made for the purpose of "obtaining or retaining business." While this sounds like legal hairsplitting, it worked—in the initial proceedings, the indictments were dismissed under exactly this logic.

But the appeals court overturned this decision and ordered a trial, on the grounds that the payments might indeed fall under the law. At that trial, the two executives were convicted, and their conviction was later upheld. The reason: the pair were found to have acted in the belief that they had to pay government officials in order to compete with companies from other parts of the world who were already doing so. The "keeping up with the Joneses" defense, which had once been successful in defending these kinds of cases, no longer applies.

The appeals court also found that it was not necessary to prove that the executives had willfully violated the terms of the FCPA itself—that is, that they knew what the law said but did otherwise anyway. In the court's ruling, a simpler standard was set out: it was enough to show that the executives knew that bribery in general was unlawful. So the "I didn't know the law" defense is out, too.

The company itself was not charged because the board of directors reported the payments to authorities as soon as they learned of them. Valuable lesson here: you can keep your company out of a lot of trouble and limit the damage caused by the poor judgment of your own employees by simply being transparent and open—rather than trying to hide the truth.

The reverse is also true: if your company does *not* do its homework and does not report what it finds, the corporation itself may land in trouble, and not merely individual employees. Also in late 2007, several companies were charged with a variety of legal violations for activities in the United Nations' oil-for-food program for Iraq. One American company was charged with violating a range of laws, including the FCPA. Culpability was established for the corporation not because the company did not have policies on its books designed to avoid engaging in corruption, but because its policies were ignored. In one instance, a simple credit check was all the due diligence needed to reveal that the overseas entity to whom it was sending payments was a shell. But warnings from midlevel people were ignored, and the company was fined tens of millions of dollars for its role in a widely publicized scandal. (Listen most closely to your people on the ground.)

THE "KEEPING UP WITH THE JONESES" ARGUMENT

Over the years American businesses have greatly lamented the "unfairness" of the Foreign Corrupt Practices Act. Usually, this centers on one basic contention: other countries' companies get away with bribery, and if we're not allowed to do the same, we're at a competitive disadvantage. These complaints have only grown louder with the increasingly global reach of Chinese businesses, which often enjoy not just a blind eye from Beijing but active support or even direction.

While businesses have been complaining about this imbalance for years, other countries' companies do *not* have a much wider playing field. In mid-2008, Siemens AG, one of Europe's largest manufacturing and technology corporations, was put on trial for an extensive "slush fund" scheme that involved over three hundred executives at the company and more than €1 billion. By late 2008, the company had been hit with over €1 billion in fines, and the Siemens reputation was permanently stained. Numerous reports have suggested that European governments, at least, are getting on the anticorruption bandwagon and aggressively enforcing international bribery and corruption laws.

The U.S. government has also gotten more aggressive about extending the FCPA to non-American firms. This is particularly important for companies in Canada and other countries that have close business ties with the United States, *especially* if their company's stock is listed on any U.S. exchanges. In 2006, a Norwegian company entered into an agreement with the U.S. government to plead guilty to violating the FCPA and paid over US$10 million in fines—even though the company is not American, the people in the bribery case were not Americans, and the bribery did not occur on U.S. soil. None of this mattered, the U.S. government argued, because the company's stock is sold on U.S. exchanges—and so the FCPA applies.

This broader interpretation comes with accelerated enforcement efforts. In 2003, branches of the U.S. government brought only two FCPA cases. In 2007, there were thirty-eight. And the first half of 2008 saw sixteen more cases, more than had ever before been logged in the first six months of any year. The trend is clear, and the costs are higher than the stories above indicate. In addition to often sizable fines, companies that are investigated often pay out millions in legal and accounting fees—as much as three times the size of the eventual fine, by some estimates, and those don't even take into account the costs of disruption and lost productivity.

COSTS OF CORRUPTION: IT'S NOT JUST THE GOVERNMENT THAT CAN GET YOU IN TROUBLE

Beyond government enforcement, there is another pitfall for companies that run afoul of corruption and bribery laws: shareholders. Increasingly, shareholders' groups are retaliating against companies that lose big by playing fast and loose with the rules. In 2007, a major biotechnology company paid US$2.5 million to settle a class-action lawsuit stemming from a bribery scandal in 2005 involving one of its European units. In 2008, another large technology firm had to make payments totaling nearly US$10 million, both to settle a shareholder suit and because of troubles caused by a kickback scandal in its Asian subsidiary. Companies (American or otherwise—if you do business in the United States, this applies to you!) that engage in bribery and other overseas corruption can find themselves rapidly bled dry by a one-two punch of zealous government prosecution and angry shareholders.

Finally, there are the bottom-line costs of bribery itself. Leading anticorruption organizations estimate that bribery worldwide adds up to about US$1 trillion per year—a substantial tax, essentially, on global business. In the worst-hit sectors, such as procurement in developing countries, the added cost of having to bribe officials to get access is similar to the imposition of a 20 percent tax on your business.

Because of all these costs, companies tend to fall into line after they get hit once—but, unfortunately, often not *before*. This is the first lesson here: learn from the mistakes of others and understand what you're doing in the international arena. Know not only what the law is, but what your own boundaries are, and stick to them.

THE CRITICAL DISTINCTION BETWEEN BRIBERY AND FACILITATION

This requires that you understand those rules, which is where the international arena is often extremely frustrating. Most of us know that outright bribery is wrong. But what about cultures where ongoing relationships are expected to be greased by certain expenditures? When is something not a bribe, but merely a "facilitating payment for routine government actions" as recognized by U.S. law as an exception to the federal corrupt practices (bribery) prohibitions? You need to understand critical distinctions here before you send your people overseas, especially if they're going to be working in cultures that have strong expectations about money and business relationships.

We make no pretense to being lawyers. We advise any company that even suspects its staff of illicit activity like this to seek competent legal counsel at once. But we can offer a few guidelines.

The difference between *bribery* and *facilitation* can be a fine one—a dangerous one. But let's look at a couple of examples. One of the core elements of bribery is solicitation: you are either asked to pay something to some individual or entity, or it is made quite plain to you that *unless* you make such a payment, you will either not realize the sale or something unpleasant will befall you. Bruce has had that game played on him for decades, especially in Third World countries.

But now let's look at things from a slightly different perspective. You have been asked to meet with the deputy minister of home affairs in the Republic of Upper Slobbovia. He is civil, even accommodating, offering you tea. You notice his suit is rather threadbare. Be assured that he knows that you are staying in the city's four-star hotel and are paying as much for a night's lodging as he earns in a month. In other words, he is very aware of the disparity between you—and envy is a powerful emotion. In this meeting, you present to him a solution to his most pressing problem: a system that completely organizes all the individual citizen data used for preparing passports and medical services. Price is not even discussed at this point. The official makes no attempt of any kind to solicit a bribe from you. In fact, he expresses reasonably serious interest in your presentation. He even asks intelligent questions. But then he tells you something that is likely true: British and German firms have presented something similar to your system, and he must obviously weigh these, too.

Are you out? No. Remember (or learn here) one of the most sovereign principles of international business: *relationship overarches the deal—always.* Should you take him out to dinner and a lap-dancer bar? Definitely not. That is not only transparent, it is often dangerous for the official to be seen in the company of a

Western executive in public. But let's say you're more observant than most Western executives in this meeting. You notice a picture of two twin girls on his desk. You ask him, "Are these your daughters?" Few and rare are the people who don't enjoy spending at least a minute talking about their own children. He will likely beam with some pride. Asking a couple more inoffensive questions, you learn that they both love outdoor sports. You have done your homework. You know that on his salary, any sports equipment is likely to be rare in his home. The next day two new soccer balls and two goal nets are delivered to his house, prepaid, with *no indication whatsoever of the donor.*

Is this bribery? Not necessarily. Although it will be for your lawyer to guide you in any particular situation, federal law does recognize as an affirmative defense that a gift was lawful under the laws of the host country. And, even in the United States, small gifts to government officials under a certain value are lawful. Also, in the situation described above, you were neither solicited for a bribe nor did the official at any time indicate that "if certain considerations are extended, your company may be favored" over your competitors. We're well aware that some purist lawyers reading this might argue otherwise, but we respectfully contend that they have not lived in the Third World, as we have. Facilitation—never in the form of cash—is as ancient a business tool as entertainment, and usually far more effective. Especially if it is a harmless gesture that makes the official look even better in the eyes of his family.

AVOIDING THE OUTSTRETCHED HANDS

You will find that some countries and areas of the world have a far higher propensity for outright bribery than others. At the moment, Africa and Latin America sit highest on this list, but the former Soviet-controlled areas are just as inclined. We are wise to remember that the Soviet system was corrupt to its very core, with even factory-floor workers being bribed by line supervisors to increase production, so that the factory could meet Moscow-dictated quotas. At a higher level, the KGB itself often bribed corrupt *apparatchiki,* or bureaucratic functionaries, to do illegal things under threat of exposure and arrest (which usually meant disappearing into a gulag in Siberia). It is wholly unrealistic of us to expect that a people raised under such a system—in which some form of petty bribery might literally have kept them or their families alive—would just suddenly throw off that yoke and embrace the American and Canadian way of doing business. Your challenge (assuming you do business in that part of the world) will be to show through a resolute sense of fairness that international business *can* successfully be done without bribery as a component.

As in so much in the business world, simple common sense can be a reliable guide in this unpleasant area of illicit requests. Think along the lines of the Golden Rule, which certainly (if practiced rightly) does not include bribery or risking the welfare of another. Call on the higher nature of the person sitting across from you. That approach is surprisingly effective.

But above all, scrutinize the character of the people you are considering sending into the less developed parts of the world. This is not hard to do (though we strongly advise against using the written assessment tests that are available). The international arena is no place for the weak in character, for they will almost assuredly bring ruin on your organization.

This reinforces a point we have made frequently throughout this book: *know your people.* If you, or somebody you trust, doesn't know the person you're about to send overseas well enough to make at least an educated guess at what that person might do if presented with a difficult situation—if asked for a bribe, for example—then your selection process has a problem. You simply must know your own people—not by spying on them (which instantly destroys morale and trust), but by developing relationships of trust over time (another reason not to send a new hire overseas immediately, unless you must—get to know this person first!). This is really an extension of good business practice—know your people, understand what they can and can't do, make sure they're being well taken care of, and build mutual trust. You'll have a lot more comfort sending people overseas on that kind of basis than sending a stranger—even with a strict policy manual—and hoping for the best.

SUMMARY

Like partnering in the previous chapter, the topic of bribery and corruption cannot be thoroughly taught in just a few pages. Learning how this works, and how to keep yourself and your company out of trouble in the overseas arena, takes more than just reading a book, even if the whole book were dedicated to that topic alone. It takes experience, and the wisdom that comes with it. If you're smart, you'll seek out people who have that experience and learn from their mistakes—and successes.

Although we don't claim to be trying to distill this wisdom into the few pages in this chapter—and we are *definitely* not making any claims to offering legal advice—we are trying to point out some basic concepts that are often overlooked or misunderstood. As with the chapter on finding trustworthy partners overseas, these long-proven concepts will give you the basics you need to start thinking about these things, and the basis for questions to ask when you do seek competent professional advice:

- For years, American businesses have claimed that the FCPA is "unfair" because it puts them at a competitive disadvantage. This has also driven many to try to get around those rules. This is no longer nearly as true as it used to be—corruption enforcement is spreading. Before you allow this logic to drive your strategy, ask yourself: if I have to engage in corruption to do business, do I really want to do this business? (We're also not averse to offering the late Peter Drucker's question: "Are you comfortable telling your wife or mother about this?")

- Corruption isn't just a law-enforcement issue. Even if you escape punishment from the government, shareholders and the general public are increasingly taking matters into their own hands. This is not a question of winning court battles, but winning over—or winning back—your shareholders and your customers.

- Bribery and facilitation are *not* the same thing. Not every expenditure is a bribe. Sometimes doing business *does* require that you scratch somebody else's back—but not in a way that's going to get you into trouble.

- Some parts of the world are more given to corruption than others. To repeat a refrain from previous chapters, *do your homework*. You should know this going in. If a demand for a bribe takes you by surprise, you weren't prepared.

- Some people are more prone to giving in on these questions than others. When you're choosing whom to send overseas, don't neglect to ask yourself what that person might do in a difficult or tempting situation. To repeat our refrain, *know your people*.

Corruption is a tremendous problem in some parts of the world, but not everywhere. A lot of international business happens daily that avoids these problems. Some of it even happens in otherwise corruption-prone areas. So the danger of corruption should not be enough to keep you from going overseas with your business. We are simply advising that you go with your eyes open, and that you be prepared to think through these issues and how your people are going to react when they do come up. One mistake in this arena can be deadly to your company. Make sure you learn from others' mistakes before you stumble into your own.

12

Send Me, Send Me!

MOST OF THIS BOOK has been written for managers—people who decide what their organization's global strategy is going to be and whom they're going to send overseas to implement it. Because we're convinced—and the data on expat-assignment failure rates are convincing—that a lot of mistakes are made here, we felt that a book to help those folks was important. We hope we've proven that point by now.

But you may not be one of those managers. Or even if you are, you yourself may want to be sent. Perhaps you regard an international posting as an important résumé-builder for your career path. (If so, go back and read chapter 8 on the perils of such thinking!) Perhaps you are looking for something new, a career adventure. Maybe you already have some international experience—study abroad in college, travel earlier in life—and want to integrate that into your career. Maybe you've already accepted the logic we laid out back in chapter 2—that now is the time to get into international business, not in spite of American and Canadian domestic economic conditions, but *because* of them. Whatever your reasons, this chapter is for you.

If this describes you, you may have jumped ahead to this chapter. If so, we urge you to go back and read what has come before. Some of it—chapters 9, 10, and 11 in particular—has valuable information about the international context that is important to anybody thinking about being involved (from whatever angle) in international business, Canadians and Americans alike. Other chapters, 3 through 6, talk about the characteristics that managers should be looking for when they are thinking about whom to send overseas to represent their company. And a couple of chapters, 7 and 8, talk about the organizational context of the company in which these decisions are made, and how that is tackled.

What we want to do here is translate all of that—especially chapters 3 through 6—into terms directly applicable to you. All of the factors and characteristics we talked about in the first part of the book are important to international business success. Some of them you have control over and can change or acquire. Some, you can't. We'll talk about the latter here and help you think through whether an international assignment is right for you. The former—what you *can* control, and how you might improve yourself and increase your chances of success internationally—we'll discuss in the next chapter.

It's important that we start with this question—is going overseas the right thing for *you?*—rather than the question many might expect or want us to address, which is, how do I convince my boss to send me? We'll get to this latter question in a bit, but for now, recall the assertion we made at the beginning of the book: *not everybody can succeed in the international arena*. The stories we've told throughout the book should be enough to convince anybody of the truth of this statement: the woman on the plane who wouldn't put on the chador, the man sent to France who refused to learn any French, the colleague who couldn't remember "Buy a donkey." In all these cases we can look back and say, clearly this was the *wrong* person for the job, and probably nothing short of sending them back to graduate school for years would correct that. And even that might not work.

So we urge you to think first not about *how* you get to go, but *whether* you should go. You want to be a success story. You don't want to end up being anecdote fodder for a future book on international business failures. So the first thing you need to commit to now is to *be honest with yourself.*

With that in mind, let's look back at the areas we discussed in our earlier chapters and think about which you can control, which you can't, and how to assess your potential for international success.

ATTITUDES TOWARD DIFFERENCES

In the academic literature on international business assignments, one consistent finding is that "cultural flexibility" or tolerance of differences is essential. This seems, to most people, to be a "duh" issue—*of course* you have to be able to deal with people who are different from you! That's like saying you have to be willing to get wet if you're going to go swimming.

But we saw in a number of stories in chapter 3 that even this most basic of observations gets violated all the time. The American banker who didn't trust Arabs. The British negotiators who looked on their Turkish counterparts as barbarians. The factory manager who demanded that Sikhs remove their wrapped turbans. There are a lot more of these kinds of stories than we want to admit, and because of them we have to deal with this issue of attitudes head-on.

Unfortunately, this is also one of the most difficult things to discuss in American and Canadian society today. While tremendous progress has been made in removing legal and institutional barriers that relegated certain groups—African-Americans, First Nations members, Hispanics—to second-class status, those efforts have also, at times, led to acrimonious conversations and serious divisions in our societies. Many in America still remember the race riots of the late 1960s, or more recently the urban anarchy and destruction following the Rodney King beating trial in 1992. Canadians may remember the mercury-poisoning scandals of First Nations communities, just as Americans recall the Tuskegee experiments, as difficult and even shameful periods in their histories. Every time a member of one of these disadvantaged groups is assaulted or shot by police, tensions flare.

Because of these difficult histories, we have a hard time dealing head-on with issues of difference, discrimination, and attitudes. Most of us, whatever our "real" feelings on the matter, have long since learned that there are publicly acceptable—and publicly unacceptable—ideas about race, gender, and diversity. Bill has seen "diversity panels" and "diversity task forces" at most of the universities and colleges he's worked for over the years, and the sad truth is that more often than not these efforts stifle open conversation rather than foster it because everybody already knows what you can and can't say in public.

So you may not have given much thought to how you feel about members of different groups, or about gender roles, or issues of religion. Chances are that you haven't had many good conversations about these things with others—especially with others who might have different perspectives. We hide what we think about differences behind the shield of social acceptability. Unfortunately, our thoughts and attitudes eventually make their way into our actions.

Now is the time to open up your own attitudes and examine them with brutal honesty. How do you feel about women and men in the workplace? Do you feel uncomfortable having to report to somebody who is a different gender or race or religion than you? Do you have problems working alongside such people?

Have you found them to be trustworthy or untrustworthy? What about as a manager—do you manage people of one race or background differently from others?

These are hard questions to answer honestly because we know what the answers *should* be. You can start by looking as objectively as you can at your own past experience. Have you had a boss or a coworker or a subordinate of a different gender, race, or religion? Was that experience uncomfortable, difficult, or did those differences not matter at all? If you can, find a trusted colleague or mentor who is also familiar with that situation and ask if she saw any difference in how you treated people—she will probably see things that you won't. Good executive coaches and mentors do this kind of thing all the time.

Another dimension to consider is, how do you feel simply *being in the minority*? If you have not had that experience before—if you didn't grow up African-American or First Nation or Hispanic or Jewish or Hindu—you may honestly not know. Most whites in the United States and Canada rarely, if ever, get to experience what it feels like to be a minority. Years ago, Bill's wife won a gift certificate to a neighborhood restaurant in Columbus, Ohio, in a charity auction. Bill and his wife had never been to that part of town before, but the place had gotten good reviews in the local papers, so they decided to check it out. The restaurant—a solidly middle-class place specializing in barbecue—was in a predominantly black section of the city. From the moment they stepped through the door, they knew that not only were they the only white folks in the room, they were the only white folks who had been there in days, possibly weeks. The service was friendly—even though the staff seemed faintly puzzled by their presence—and the food superb. But by the time he walked out that night, Bill had gotten a small taste of something that college and graduate school and the rest of his life experience had never given him: what it felt like to be a small minority in a community of difference. Similarly, when Bruce lived for a number of years in South Africa, he was never unconscious that he was part of a 10 percent minority (the whites) in a country primarily of blacks.

How will you react to that situation? How will it make you feel, and how will it affect your behavior toward others? The old saying "You'll never know until you try" applies here. If you *have* had those experiences before, now is the time to reflect on them. If you haven't, before you accept any international assignment—before you even put yourself in for one—go get some. Take a trip overseas, or into a community very different from yours. Spend some time there. Make it as immersive as you can. Don't fly to Acapulco and stay in the tourists-only area. If you've acquired some language skills (see below), try them out. See how you react when you're the only one around like you. If you find this an intensely uncomfortable experience, going international may not be for you.

This is also a good time to examine your own core values. Do you have coherent thoughts about gender roles? What are your thoughts about religion—both yours and others? Some religious value systems are by their nature extremely tolerant. Bill has a devout Hindu colleague who is probably the most religiously tolerant person he's ever met because his theology essentially subsumes all other religions. Other religious traditions are stricter, with claims about right and wrong paths. Where are *your* beliefs, and will they affect how you interact with other people in the workplace?

Canada is a bilingual country—two official languages. Switzerland is quadralingual—four official languages. But South Africa has *eleven* official languages. Bruce lived for nine years in South Africa and had made many trips there before his long-term residency, often for a month or more at a time. From his very first visit, quite some years back, he was struck by what he finally decided was a needless fear among whites of entering many of the black township areas. From then on Bruce went in and out of many townships without incident. Not once did he encounter resistance or even the semblance of a threat to his safety. Was it because of his audacity in entering? No. Definitely not. It was because of his attitude toward the black South Africans living there. As we've stressed at several points in this book, *you will be a minority no matter where you are sent overseas to live and work*. You must every day be mindful of your guest status. Show respect for your host people's ways. Never forget that they can sense insincerity in a heartbeat! (Can't you?)

The etymology of the word *tolerance* is, not surprisingly, from Latin. But its modern form and usage come from late Middle English. Across the centuries since its absorption into English, the word has referred to one's ability to endure hardship. Make no mistake: sometimes it *will* be a hardship to tolerate certain customs and practices of your overseas hosts. But tolerance is one of the higher-toned ideas of the civilized mind: a tolerant mind genuinely recognizes the good to be had from respecting the coexistence of different ways of thinking and living. As it was put by the American philosopher Harry Overstreet early in the last century, tolerance is the hallmark of the mature mind.

Keep in mind, too, that if you are genuinely uncomfortable with certain kinds of differences, that doesn't automatically disqualify you from *all* international assignments. We made this point in various ways in chapter 3—different kinds of difference matter in different places. In much of the world, being Jewish is a nonfactor, but in some parts of the Muslim Middle East, it's critical. If you're uncomfortable working with women in positions of authority, northern Europe could be problematic, but Latin America or Japan may well not be. And if strong male ideas about gender roles are bothersome (as was true for our colleague in Peru, trying to dine alone), the opposite may be true.

The bottom line here is, you need to *honestly* assess how you feel about major dimensions of differences—gender, race, religion—both socially and in the workplace. Get a trusted friend or outsider (*not* your boss!) to help you with this, because she will help you see parts of yourself that you can't. Don't put in for an international assignment in a part of the world where your values or beliefs are going to get you into trouble. Make sure that your views and values match those of the place you want to be sent. Don't set yourself up for failure.

LANGUAGE

This may be the biggest barrier to Canadians and Americans in going overseas. Fear of learning a foreign language ranks up there with fear of math for most of us. There's an old joke in international circles: A person who speaks three languages is trilingual. A person who speaks two languages is bilingual. A person who speaks only one language is an American!

But Canadians have their own challenges. From Andrea Mandel-Campbell's book again:

> The [Canadian] government should follow the lead of the Edmonton public school system, which offers seven bilingual programs and is widely considered one of the best school systems in the world. Unfortunately, the prospects aren't promising. According to Ontario provincial legislation, it is illegal to offer bilingual programs in languages other than English and French. When the Toronto school board was asked whether it was open to introducing a similar program, the answer was that it would be 'difficult,' because it wouldn't be fair to the hundreds of other world languages that weren't chosen. 'Equity is a big thing at the school board,' said one rep. 'Which language would you choose?' (Gee, maybe the one parents ask for?) That's almost as much of a disservice as the one done to Quebecers who are denied the right to learn English, which is still the world's predominant business language. Several Québec entrepreneurs I spoke with told me that

their lack of English-language skills had been a huge disadvantage, and as a result they had made sure to send their children to
English universities.[1]

As we pointed out in chapter 4, for some people this fear is
well-founded. Some people simply have no gift for language, even
at the most basic level. If our colleague couldn't learn to repeat
"Buy a donkey," the chances of his learning anything more complicated than how to say "thank you" were slim to none. If you
are one of these people, you need to know that now, and you
probably need to avoid the international arena like the plague!

Language is also, as we argued in chapter 4, an issue of attitude. Some people *could* learn, but refuse to do so. As with attitudes toward difference, you need to be brutally honest with
yourself in this area. If you're not willing to learn a language,
know that. If you think everybody else in the world should speak
English, admit it. Mark Twain captured this well in a dialogue
between Huck Finn and the Negro Jim, as they puzzled over
Frenchmen. After establishing that cats and cows don't talk like
people, because they're different creatures, Jim was confused. "Is a
Frenchman a man, Huck?" he asks his friend. "Then why don't he
talk like a man?"

If you feel like Jim, you probably don't belong in the international arena. But in our experience, most people *can* learn another
language, or at least enough to do what they need to do. This
starts with basic politeness. If you can learn a few phrases—
please, *thank you*, *yes*, *no*, and forms of address—you'll be off to
a roaring start. As we pointed out in chapter 4, in many parts of
the world, the rewards even for this are tremendous, because so

---

1. Andrea Mandel-Campbell, *Why Mexicans Don't Drink Molson: Rescuing Canadian Business from the Suds of Global Obscurity* (Vancouver, BC:
Douglas & McIntyre, 2007), 304.

few outsiders will take the time to try it. (Please enjoy practicing some of the key phrases in several different languages that you'll find at the end of this book.)

Here you need to assess seriously the needs of the job you're considering. Will you be sent to a small city in China for three years? Then learning Chinese to a reasonable degree of fluency is going to be necessary. If, however, the job takes you to Hong Kong for short stints, you may be able to get by mostly with English, with some basic Chinese phrases, and common sense (such as carrying a phrase book) to use as appropriate. Whom will you be dealing with? A large American marketing firm sent one of its executives to meet with a team of people from a French marketing company. Unfortunately, nobody thought to ask about language ahead of time—on either side. The American spoke and understood no French at all, while the French team's English was extremely weak. Naturally, the meeting was a complete waste of time and money. If *either* side had thought ahead to inquire about the language requirements of the other, the result could have been quite different. So if you are considering an international posting, find out what the needs will be, then consider whether you are willing to meet those requirements.

Luckily, unless you fall into that small category of people who cannot learn other languages at all, you can increase your capabilities in this area—if you are motivated enough. Over the years in his working career, Bruce has learned several languages, including Russian, Bulgarian, Turkish, Spanish, French, German, and Afrikaans—some through formal study, some through self-teaching. Bill studied German formally, learned basic Afrikaans informally, and has picked up just enough Zulu to be polite in key situations. Most of us carry around at least a few phrases in another language, even if we don't think about it much—rare is the Anglophone Canadian who cannot say *bonjour* or the American who hasn't watched enough *Sesame Street* to say *gracias* and *buenos días*. These are foundations that you can build on. The rewards, in goodwill and the opening of minds and hearts around the world, are tremendous.

ATTITUDES TOWARD DIFFERENT WAYS OF DOING THINGS

We talked in chapter 5 about the danger of "missionary impulses" in the international business arena. By this we didn't necessarily mean religiously motivated missionaries, but people who are uncomfortable with different cultures and societies and who try to change them to be more "like us" or "like proper civilization." Missionaries come in a wide variety of types, but as we pointed out in chapter 5, they're all deadly to success in the international arena.

This is less of an issue of dealing with different kinds of people than it is dealing with different *behaviors*. If you're uncomfortable working with Asians, or having a woman as a supervisor, that may affect your job performance, but you don't expect your coworkers to stop being Asians or your supervisor to stop being female. Being a missionary means trying to *change* the way others do things—which often, to them, means changing who they are.

In this area, experience matters. We tend not to know what kinds of behaviors or ways of running things or interacting with others really bother us until we encounter them. If you have spent most or all of your life in the United States or Canada, and within your home country primarily in communities and groups that are familiar to you, you may not have a very good idea of how you'll react in a situation where things are done very differently. If you cannot function without morning coffee, working will be difficult in some parts of the world. If you *have* to have meals at certain times of the day, you had better make sure that the place you're going to shares that schedule—which many places won't.

Much of this falls under the general heading of "cultural

adaptability." Scores of articles and books discuss this topic (we've listed some of the better ones in our "Recommended Reading" list at the end of this book), and it's widely acknowledged that to be successful in the international business arena, you have to be able to adapt to the quirks of other cultures (bowing instead of shaking hands, always taking and giving business cards with both hands, eating late, that sort of thing). We support and agree with this literature and advise you to go read some of it. Use it to help get a sense of your own "cultural adaptability index."

However, the unexamined dimension here is not cultural practices, but *business* practices. Many American and Canadian businessmen will develop a taste for new foods, learn a bit of the local language, and pride themselves on their ability to move easily from one social milieu to another. But those same people, when it comes to business, will become adamant that business be done their way, because their way is the *right* way. The missionary impulse often causes the most damage in international business here: the desire to teach "them" how "business is really done."

One of the services we offer our clients is especially enjoyable for us. We take between three and five CEOs, organization chiefs, or key vice presidents on a special tour of just a few countries. We select those countries according to the common interests of these clients and put them together for the entire tour. We also promise each of them one appointment with a high-level government official and one with the CEO of a company with whom they might work well in each country—either in a joint venture or perhaps in some other profitable arrangement. Before we leave, they are all immersed in a pretty serious study of the most important things to know about each country: cultural taboos, good practices, their belief systems, the history—and some of the language. So, when they get to each country, they are way ahead of the pack. With few exceptions, this has worked flawlessly over the years, with most coming home with new deals or partnerships.

But, oh, those few exceptions . . . On one trip, we were invited for dinner to a Saudi sheikh's home. Now remember that each of the American executives had been thoroughly briefed on the do-and-don't scenarios in this country. Nevertheless, not long after we had been seated, one of the Americans looked around the room and realized that only men were present. Suddenly he loudly insisted that the sheikh's wives and daughters be brought in to the dinner, even though he had been warned that this was never ever done in Saudi society, for strong religious and cultural reasons. Bruce hastened to tender an apology on the executive's behalf, and things appeared to settle down. But only for about ten minutes. Then came the explosive phrase "Hey, this lamb is really good, but don't you think it'd be even better with a nice Cabernet Sauvignon?" This one American executive ruined all prospects for the rest of his teammates as well as himself.

On another trip, we had only one client along with us, who had already begun a small-business undertaking in newly liberated Bulgaria. He, too, had been well briefed. He was having trouble with some corrupt customs officials (at that time an evil inherited from the old Soviet days), which we were diligently but quietly working to resolve. We were meeting with the president of Bulgaria for coffee that evening (Bruce was at that time also a special adviser to the president). So we warned the American again: Bulgarians are a very compartmentalized people. Nobody wants you to disclose problems with one part of your life to another not directly involved with your problem. Yes, you guessed it—within five minutes the American was using expletives in decrying the corrupt customs officials to the president of the country. Bruce was calculating if he might fit under the carpet! He was able to rescue the affair, but not without deep anguish and embarrassment. Fortunately, the president was a man of remarkable tolerance! If you're set on being posted overseas, leave the missionary zeal at home in North America!

If you want to be honest about your fitness for going overseas, you need to examine your own ideas about *how* you get business done. Can you adapt to different practices? Would it drive you crazy to work in an environment where women and men will not mix at business dinners? Where alcohol is never served? Or where you can't just scream to a country's president to "fix" your business problem? Are you goal-oriented or process-oriented? If the process is really critical to you, you will want to restrict yourself to parts of the world where your business process is accepted practice and avoid places where things are done differently.

This is not to say that the locals are always right, either. Sometimes ways of doing business in other societies—particularly in the developing world—*are* dysfunctional. Sometimes you may have to buck those trends to accomplish your company's goals. Figuring out when to do so, and which lines can and can't be crossed in a given culture, takes a great deal of business cultural fluency, which can only be learned over time and with experience. If you're just starting out or are still early in your international business career, you won't have that yet. That's okay; you'll develop it, in the same way every other successful international businessman does: over time, and by learning from your failures and successes. The point we're making is not that you have to have that level of fluency now. But you do have to have the tools with which to develop it. Being able to understand and adapt to different ways of doing business is one of those fundamental tools. Without it, you will learn nothing, no matter how many experiences you have. Make sure you understand your own makeup here, and if you don't think you can adjust beyond certain lines, don't try to force the issue. As we'll discuss below, you can control certain things about yourself, but not everything—and trying to control something that you really can't is almost always a recipe for failure.

UNDERSTANDING AND ADAPTING TO TIME DIFFERENCES

As we discussed back in chapter 6, the question of time in international business has several dimensions. Any of them can cause serious problems. While we don't often think about time—most of our routines are automatic—if you're considering being sent overseas, you need to think about how time issues affect you.

Maybe the simplest—but also often the most vexing—is translating across time zones. The mathematics involved are simple: adding and subtracting numbers up to twenty-four, which most children can do by the time they're eight. But some people have tremendous difficulty getting their minds to do these calculations quickly, or remembering to do them at all. Both of us have been awakened in the middle of the night by people who forgot about the time difference, or who miscalculated it. Even within Canada and the United States, which run four or five time zones from one end to the other, people sometimes have difficulty remembering the time differential between Vancouver and Boston, or Los Angeles and Montréal. If you are one of these people, you need to either train yourself out of it (more on this below) or stay out of the international arena.

Jet lag is another factor that has to be experienced to be understood. If you've never flown seven time zones away, you can't know how that will affect your body and your mind. As we mentioned in chapter 6, some people are hardly affected at all (Bill falls into this category, to the point that his kids refer to it as his "secret mutant superpower"), while others are knocked for a loop for days on end. If you're strongly affected by jet lag, this doesn't necessarily disqualify you from going overseas. You can mitigate the effects on your business performance in many ways, mostly by giving yourself plenty of recovery time after you arrive and before you have to really start working. However, if the assignment calls for constant shuttling back and forth, with relatively short stays and not much recovery time, that may not be for you. How do you know? Think back on your own travel experiences or test yourself on some trips. Follow some of the tips we gave back in chapter 6 and see if you can recover quickly. Be honest with yourself!

Finally, there's the question of *time expectations*. This is really a subset of the cultural-adaptability issue we talked about above. Some people are very dependent on particular schedules: breakfast at 0630h, dinner at 1800h, teatime at 1600h. Others can adjust their schedule to the demands of the day, but need things to be done *on time*—meetings must start promptly, deadlines must be met, people have to call when they say they will call. As we've discussed throughout the book, the rest of the world doesn't necessarily meet our expectations in these ways. Many cultures (Portuguese and Middle Eastern for example) are used to eating evening meals much later than is typical in the United States or Canada. Others (such as Cyprus) will linger much longer over a meal. People who have done business in Latin America or Africa will tell you that meetings rarely start on time—often not even on the *day* they were scheduled for—unlike the punctuality of Germany or Switzerland.

Here is a story from our own experiences that illustrates several of our points with regard to the importance of tolerating differences in seeing time, adaptability, tolerance, and boldness. Some years back, when Bruce was an international-marketing manager for a British multinational firm, the company was in a final competitive struggle to sell its tactical-communications system to the ministry of defense of a key Latin American country. Bruce's competitor was a major French company. The prices being offered by Bruce's firm and the French firm were nearly the same. The technical specifications were almost identical. Bruce had scheduled a meeting with the minister of defense to discuss the issue. But at the appointed time that Monday morning, he was told that the minister had not come to the capital city that day, after all. So another meeting was set for Wednesday afternoon. But again, when Bruce showed up, he was told that the minister was occupied and would see him "in a few hours." Those hours passed, the sun went down—and the minister apparently left out the back door. (As we said elsewhere in this book, this completely different view of time and appointments is very common in several parts of the world.)

Undaunted, Bruce learned the next day through sympathetic secretaries that the minister was at his hacienda many hours distant from the capital city. (*Always* treat secretaries and personal assistants with honor and respect; they can be your best friends!) So Bruce boarded a noisy 1940s-vintage bus with a ton of cargo strapped sloppily to the roof. On the long, dusty, steaming hot ride out of town, Bruce ended up holding a chicken on his lap. For hours. Finally he reached the target town and got the locals to identify the minister's hacienda. Drenched with perspiration, covered with road dust, he approached the gates. The guards predictably refused him entry, but one finally called inside. Moments later Bruce was sitting on a lovely shaded veranda, sipping a cold sangría with the minister, who was smiling and gracious—and completely unapologetic. "Minister, I've come with a couple of thoughts about your dilemma on the systems," Bruce began, but the minister held up a hand to stop him. "*Compramos su sistema!*" he told the astonished Bruce. They're buying *our* system? "*Oh, yo no había conocido eso,*" replied Bruce. (Oh, I had not known that.) The minister smiled and raised his glass. "*Oye, usted apareció!*" (Hey, you showed up!)

We mentioned several chapters ago the American philosopher who remarked, "The success is in the boldness!" We encourage you to experiment when you are overseas, but only after you have acquired some serious experience in your new culture. Bruce was not new at the international game when he ventured to the minister's private hacienda. He had a lot of experience under his belt before he dared to experiment with the system a bit. He also never once accused the minister of "disrespecting" his time or avoiding him. There is a critical difference here between respecting the host culture and being willing to push boundaries and rules a bit. The key is to *respect the person, and let him know it.* That can give you some room to push a little bit, especially against unwritten rules about where meetings should take place or how they should be arranged. Don't fear experimentation like this, but make sure you're ready—you should be *thoroughly* familiar with the culture. Carry that chicken on your lap. Then expect success.

In this area of dealing with different understandings of time, you don't necessarily have to go overseas first to see what your strengths and weaknesses are. We've all had experiences with delayed meetings and disrupted schedules. Think back on those times—how did you react? Did it throw off your productivity for the day? Were you angry? Did other things suffer because of the schedule change? Or were you able to adapt your work flow to the new circumstances and continue to get things done? Here again, it will pay off to ask a trusted friend or mentor for *his* view as well—he may see reactions in you that you don't see in yourself. In a domestic workplace, struggling to cope with shifted schedules is a challenge. In the international arena, where the disruptions and changes are going to be orders of magnitude greater, it can mean the difference between success and failure. If you have to have a predictable and ordered schedule to be productive, international assignments are probably not the right path for you, unless they're in western or northern Europe.

SUMMARY: DO YOUR HOMEWORK!

We can't emphasize enough that if you are interested in being sent overseas, you have to do a serious assessment of yourself as well as the available opportunities. We've been pushing managers throughout this book to do the same when they consider whom to send: make sure they're sending the right people. This is your chance to help do their jobs for them, by making sure you really are the right person.

This calls for an honest assessment of your strengths and weaknesses across the dimensions we outlined above:

- How comfortable—or uncomfortable—are you with differences? How much are you affected by differences in race, gender, religion? Can you productively work with, or under, people very different from you?
- Can you learn a foreign language? Are you *willing* to learn a foreign language? How far are you willing to go—just enough to be polite, or to gain conversational fluency?
- Can you work with different ways of doing business? Do certain practices drive you to distraction? Are you seized with a strong desire to change the way others do things?
- How much time flexibility do you have? Can you think and operate across multiple time zones? Do you get seriously jet-lagged? How wedded are you to your daily routine?

You want to think these things through, first of all for yourself. Getting sent abroad if you're not prepared can be a career-damaging, even career-ending, move. But if you go through this process and become convinced—by evidence that you can corroborate with others—that you *are* well suited to the international environment, you will have a much stronger case to make with your employer that you should be the one to go.

13

I've Got What It Takes—
Now What?

WE'LL ASSUME THAT YOU'VE been through the preceding chapter. You've had the honest conversation with yourself; thought through your strengths and weaknesses across the various areas we discussed; and gotten feedback from trusted mentors and colleagues to corroborate (or challenge) your findings. You've held yourself up against the image we've presented of what it takes to be a successful internationalist, and you're convinced that you fit the bill.

That's great! The world needs people like you, for lots of reasons, many of which we've already outlined. Businesses and organizations are increasingly forced to go global, both by current circumstances and by broader ongoing forces that aren't going to change anytime soon. As we've argued from the beginning, that means they need people who can do it well. If you are one of those people, you've got a bright future ahead of you.

But just because you have the root characteristics for success overseas doesn't mean that you are ready to get on the next plane, or that you can't improve. Recall another point we've made throughout the book: international work is very dependent on where you are going and what you are going to do. Even if you have the things we discussed in the last chapter, there's still plenty of preparation that can make you better—and prove to your employer that you're the indispensable person for the job.

IMPROVING YOURSELF: DO YOUR HOMEWORK FIRST

Having done a serious self-examination of your strengths and weaknesses, you know what kinds of difference you are and aren't comfortable with. You know how much of a language gap you are prepared to cross, and what skills you already have. You understand your level of flexibility with regard to working with different business practices. You know your own internal clock and expectations of time, and how much change you can tolerate. You think—in your most honest assessment—that you have enough of what it takes to be posted overseas. And you are still motivated—you really *want* to go. Now what?

Chances are good that you are stronger in some of the areas discussed in the previous chapter than in others. Few of us, especially early in our careers, have all the tools we need to succeed—we acquire many of them along the way. If we're smart, we try to do so intentionally, developing new talents and abilities that will help get us to where we want to go (in this case, overseas). So if you're really bent on going overseas, what can you work on, and what do you have to accept?

First, we repeat, *know the requirements of the job.* Do your homework. Where will this position be and what are the conditions like over there? What's the business culture? What are common expectations regarding time? How are differences of race, gender, religion, belief, and practice treated? What's the local attitude toward Westerners? If you're serious about being posted abroad, you need to thoroughly research these things. By the time you are ready to go—preferably, by the time you apply—you should be *the* company expert on that location. Somebody who can persuasively argue that she understands German culture and practice—and how these affect the business—is going to be much more convincing than somebody who simply points to the two years of German on his college transcript.

A part of this homework is *understanding the nature of the job*. Is this a long-term assignment? Will you be based in one place, or will you have to travel around a lot? Will you need to take your family with you, and if so, what will things be like for them? Whom will you be working with, and how much exposure have those folks had to Canadians and Americans in general, and to your company's practices in particular? There's a big difference between going abroad for a few months to work in a well-established office with locals who have spent a lot of time at the headquarters in Sioux City or Saskatoon (and who are already employed by your company), and being the first person to go abroad to set up a new operation and chase clients who may never have heard of your product! You can only evaluate your strengths and weaknesses relative to what you would be asked to do.

LEARN THE LANGUAGE

Once you've done your homework and figured out what you need to develop to make yourself more "sendable," then what? Assuming that you have *some* aptitude—and as we've pointed out, some people don't, no matter how hard they try—learning a foreign language may be one of the easier and more controllable things you can do. If you're serious about going overseas, build your language skills. If you want to make a case to your boss or your employer that you're the one who should go to the new partnership office in France, emphasize your French-language skills (if you have them) or offer to acquire some—and demonstrate that commitment by beginning work immediately. The primary barrier to learning new languages is not the actual difficulty—certainly, it takes time, but young children do it all the time, in every language on earth—but attitude, and that is well within your control.

Bruce has spent a lot of time in Switzerland. The country hosts five languages: French, Italian, Romansch, and *two* forms of German (the high German used in Germany and Austria, and Schwiitzertüütsch, a separate Swiss German that Austrians call a throat disease, for its many guttural words). As a dinner guest in the homes of several Swiss families, Bruce has observed their very young children at table. Almost always the child will excitedly speak in a mix of two or three languages in the same sentence. The Swiss long ago learned (as confirmed by Piaget and others) that all the parents have to do is answer the child in whichever language is dominant in the child's sentence. It's that simple and that natural. Within months the child is able to make the differentiations necessary to speak only in one language or the other.

When studying a language, take care. One simple consonant can make a heck of a difference. When Bruce was fairly new in using Spanish conversationally, he wondered why in Latin America he was so often asked if he was tired. What they were really asking was "Are you married?" (*¿Está usted casado?*) He heard it as *cansado*—tired. So in response to the question about being married, he would reply, "No, thank you, I slept quite well last night!"

DEVELOPING FLEXIBILITY: HOW FAR CAN YOU BEND?

If you find yourself uncomfortable around some kinds of people who are different from you, you can try to work on this also—to a point. Tolerance for differences is more difficult to change strategically, although not impossible. This will depend on *why* you feel uncomfortable around some other kinds of people. If the discomfort is primarily because of lack of exposure—a vague sense of unease simply because "I've never had a nonwhite supervisor before" or "I've never worked on a team where a woman was in charge," that may be fixable, *if* the novelty is the sole source of the problem. People who have enough innate flexibility can adapt to novelty. But if your discomfort is linked to more deep-seated convictions—if you have strong views about the roles of women and men in society, or the relationships among different religious faiths, or a genuinely deep dislike for people of other groups or races—trying to change will likely only lead to disaster. Parts of us can be pretty flexible, but we all carry around a core set of feelings, beliefs, and ideals that is tampered with only at great peril. If working across differences is treading on that core, trying to change it simply to fit the demands of a job is almost certainly a big—and costly—mistake.

This also goes for your flexibility on business practices. If the issue is merely that you need a little adjustment time to get used to a different way of doing business, fine. In preparation for an overseas assignment, try to get as much exposure to the novel practice as you can, so you can start adjusting to it. On the other hand, you may simply not be able to work with some business tendencies, and for good reasons. If your company wants to work in a culture where quality control simply can't be done, because "that's not the way they do things," and your company's main claim to fame is the quality of its products—maybe it's not you that needs to change, but your company's strategy. So in the realm of adapting to business practices, take a good, close look at *why* you find a particular way of doing things problematic. Is it possible to do things their way and still accomplish your company's goals? If so, can you adapt to doing it their way instead of yours? If the answers are yes, then work on broadening your style. If the answer to the first question is no, suggest that the company shouldn't go there—and if they do anyway, stay away! And if the answer to the second question is no, don't push yourself for the assignment—you're not the right person for that job.

Finally, time flexibility can, to some degree, be learned with practice. Maybe you find translating across time zones difficult because you've never done it much. If so, start practicing and see how easy you find it. Similarly, if the job is going to require very different kinds of daily schedules, experiment with those. See if you can train yourself to work productively even though you're getting up earlier—or later—than you're used to, and eating meals at different times. If you've done a good assessment of yourself, you may already have tried some of this—now's the time to work on it seriously. The more you can adjust before the wheels go up, the smoother your transition will be on the other end.

We obviously can't give a complete list of things to do here. We don't know where you're going, we don't know what your organization will ask you to do, and we don't know *you*. But if you've done your homework, *you* know all these things or will soon. To help you prepare, we've included a list of suggested readings and materials in the back of this book. Pick the ones most helpful to your situation, and work hard!

SUMMARY: BE THE BEST YOU CAN BE

We can't emphasize enough that if you are interested in being sent overseas as a significant career path, you have to do a serious assessment of yourself as well as the opportunities you might be sent into. We've been pushing managers throughout this book to do the same when they consider whom to send: make sure you're sending the right people. This is your chance to help do managers' jobs for them, by making sure you really are the right person, and if you are, by preparing yourself as well as you can. If you have gone through a thorough and honest self-examination and think you've got what it takes to be successful overseas, the next step is to prepare yourself in those dimensions that you have control over:

- Do your external homework: learn everything you can about the host country and business environment. Become the company go-to expert.
- Do your internal homework: thoroughly understand what your company is asking you to do.
- Test your flexibility to different situations, different times, and different ways of doing things. Start practicing now.
- Work on your language skills. If you're starting fresh, learn the basics you know you'll need. If you have a base in the language already, brush it up. Practice, practice, practice.

14

Start with the Basics and Get It Right

WE'VE MADE THE ARGUMENT throughout this book that globalizing a business or organization rests, more than anything else, on *whom you send*. This shouldn't come as a surprise. No matter how large and complex our companies and institutions become, everything ultimately boils down to individual people getting things done together. Although "people are our most important resource" has become a cliché, it is no less true for that. Everyone with almost any experience—in business, in nonprofit organizations, in running a local school bake sale—knows that success hinges on getting the right people into the right places, doing the right things.

Accomplishing this in a *global* context, unfortunately, is much more complicated. It takes us away from what we know and puts us into the realm of the unknown. Old habits and practices don't work, and we have things to think about that, in the familiar business at home, we've never before had to consider. But the world outside of North America is, in a word, *different*. So we have to do things differently.

We've talked about a lot of ways the overseas world is different. Some of these things, such as learning another language, are obvious, although that doesn't keep people from messing them up. Others—issues of race and gender, for example—may look familiar but actually play out very differently in other parts of the world. And still others—such as time differences, physical and cultural—are wholly new. In covering all of these areas, we hope we've given you useful tips and important pointers of what to look for and what to consider.

But through all of this complexity, some simple points emerge. While the world is complicated, the fundamentals of global business aren't really that complex. We started the book with an important statement about the individuals that you choose to send abroad: *not everybody can do this*. We still firmly believe that, because we've had many, many years to observe it. Some people in every organization should probably not be sent overseas. But that does *not* mean that organizations cannot be successful, regardless of their size or type or mission. We also believe that *every organization and every company can get this right*. If we didn't, we wouldn't have written this book.

So what are the fundamentals of getting global business right? Here, we need to make some distinctions, because the important lessons will depend on who you are and where you fit into the larger organization. We've made references to these different groups throughout the book, and we understand that what you get out of this depends on where you fit in the larger picture.

FOR EXECUTIVES AND MANAGERS

It's possible that you're reading this book because your organization is in the early stages of thinking about how to globalize itself.

A lot of companies are doing that these days, given the severe domestic market problems in the United States and Canada. So this book may simply be a part of your reading list as you're thinking about how to globalize. Obviously this isn't the end of that list—no one book could be!—but it does address one element that no one else does.

If you're in this situation, we urge you to remember one point, even if you remember nothing else: *it all starts with people.* Especially when you're starting a new partnership or a new venture, face-to-face meetings are critical. Even the ones that take place on your home turf are, in essence, international meetings. How you handle these initial person-to-person contacts is crucial—and *whom* you have handling them is even more so.

So if you're just starting out, don't let the big dreams and strategic plans—as important as those are—get in the way of focusing on the people part now. Ask yourself, do I have the right people to do this? How will I identify them? If we don't already have them, can we go find some or develop them from the people we've already got? If you write your grand strategy and then at the last minute go hunting for people to execute it, you're likely to run into trouble. The best strategy in the world won't save you from poor execution, as every seasoned executive knows.

Another important lesson is *apply this to yourself and your management colleagues.* Often organizations think it necessary to send the "big guns" to the "important" meetings. This violates one of Peter Drucker's famous dictums: "Most discussions of decision making assume that only senior executives make decisions or that only senior executives' decisions matter. This is a dangerous mistake." So before you send yourself overseas to meet with that new partner, go back and read the previous two chapters written for your employees. If you're not the right person for the job, *don't go.*

This gets even trickier when your new partners are visiting you. Clearly, meetings with senior management on the home field are important—but so are first impressions. When you're playing host, the question isn't whether you meet with your foreign guests—it's how you manage that visit. Here again, *you need to size up your own strengths and weaknesses*. If you're not the right person to handle such a meeting, find someone who is. Or limit your role and turn over a lot of the key details to a seasoned internationalist.

Back in chapter 7 we told you the story of Bruce's managing that huge technical system connected to the evacuation of the Sinai. One of the company's senior executives was a fond adherent of the naïve American belief that "we're all the same"—arguably the most dangerously false assumption anyone who touches the international world can make. The Egyptian government sent three senior advisers—all Egyptians—to spend a week observing the progress. On their second day there, the senior executive decided to take them all to lunch—at a BBQ restaurant known for exclusively serving pork. By showing no respect for *their* beliefs this executive gave obvious and deep offense that was immediately seen by the three Muslims. It took Bruce considerable effort to restore the *overall sense of trust* that had been compromised by so thoughtless a gesture.

It *is* possible to do this right—if you remember that, even though you're on your home turf, you still have to respect the other side. Some years ago, Bill was working for a university that had an exchange relationship with a university in Japan. Two Japanese officials were coming to visit Bill's campus—it was the first visit for the senior Japanese administrator of the team. In his position, Bill knew he would have to meet several times with the Japanese guests, so he did his homework. He learned a few simple Japanese phrases—*konnichiwa* (good day), *domo arigato* (thank you), *sayonara* (goodbye). He brushed up on basic elements of politeness, knowing that small gestures of courtesy are very important to the Japanese. He prepared himself to give and receive business cards with both hands, to bow slightly upon greeting, and to give and receive gifts. In all, he spent perhaps two hours preparing for the meetings.

The investment paid off handsomely. When the guests arrived, they were a bit lost in the large building and unsure of where to go to their first meeting. When Bill called out, *"Konnichiwa, Asano-san!"* they were instantly put at ease. The small phrases and courtesies throughout the meal and subsequent meetings eased the tension and helped the guests feel comfortable—even when Bill's boss, rather than handing her business card to the visitors, slid it across the table casually! By the end of the visit, the lead guest asked Bill if he had ever been to Tokyo and was surprised to learn that he had never been to Japan! These small things could easily have been ignored because the meetings were in the United States. But it was still an international meeting, and the same rules that we've discussed throughout the book apply. This is not hard! We just need to do our homework, and be thoughtful of others.

Maybe international operation isn't a new thing to you. Perhaps your organization is already operating in the global arena, but you've run into problems. Maybe you're not getting the returns you expected, or perhaps you've got programs that aren't running smoothly and achieving their goals. Organizations facing trouble often look to tweak the game plan first: Do we need to change strategies? Adopt a different tactic? Use different measurements or different incentives? Should we renegotiate the arrangement?

When things go wrong, unless it's an obvious personnel failure, we seldom ask, *do I have the right people involved?* Think back on many of the stories we've relayed throughout the book. In a few cases, the cause of the failure would be obvious to you, sitting back at headquarters. But in many cases, it wouldn't—especially if your primary source of information about how the business meeting went or how things were going on the ground was the person himself. We made a point of saying in chapter 10, trust your people.

But you have to have done your homework first and made sure you have the *right* people.

So if you're having difficulties in your international operations, take a careful look to see if you've got the right people in place. Have someone in your company who knows them well assess them—and have them assess themselves and their overseas experience—along the lines that we've discussed throughout the book. The answer may become clear. Maybe your people haven't learned how to deal with the locals' sense of time and keep scheduling meetings in the wrong way. Maybe they have attitudes or habits that would clearly turn off potential partners. Maybe they're just not cut out for the international arena (in which case, chances are good they're pretty unhappy about how it's going!).

This shouldn't be an inquisition. That they're not doing well in the international arena doesn't mean that they're bad people. We have known many bright and highly effective people who are, for various reasons, lost at sea when they go abroad. That doesn't make them bad employees. It just means that they were ill-placed. As Peter Drucker reminded us repeatedly, the productivity of the worker is not the responsibility of the *worker*, but of the *manager*.

FOR HUMAN RESOURCES PROFESSIONALS

As we pointed out back in chapter 7, human resources has a tremendously important role to play in identifying and selecting the right people for overseas work. HR often gets tasked with a lot of administrative detail—benefits paperwork, running calculations on comparative salary and compensation packages, maintaining personnel files. All of these are important and need to be done. But in the realm we're talking about, HR has an even more vital role: *facilitating the honest conversations* that need to take place.

For organizations large enough to have their own HR offices, this is likely not only important but necessary. Who else in a large organization has information about your existing pool of talent? Who else is tasked with the primary responsibility for developing and organizing that talent and has the professional training and skill to do so? Executives and managers, though they need to think about whom to send (see above), also need to think about lots of other things: setting strategic goals, deploying other kinds of resources, dealing with outside stakeholders, and managing ongoing projects.

This puts HR in the perfect position to bring to bear the important perspectives we laid out in chapters 3 through 6, and to facilitate the kinds of conversations we talked about in chapter 7. You are in the ideal location to understand the needs of a particular international assignment—which the manager or executive undoubtedly knows well—and incorporate that with what we've been talking about in this book. Indeed, if *you* read this book but your executives don't, you have crucial information that could make the difference between success and failure—on dimensions that the executive level hasn't even thought of yet!

So for all the references we made throughout the book to *know your people* and *have honest conversations*, this is where HR can bring tremendous value to the process. How this happens will be different in every organization, of course, but that it needs to happen cannot be disputed. Maybe you incorporate it into an annual evaluation process, or even into the hiring and intake procedures—the earlier you can identify people with international aptitudes, the better. Maybe you make a habit of having regular conversations with personnel who might be interested in going overseas to talk through some of these issues. If you know your organization is likely to be looking for people for overseas assignments, you can be proactive—and make your contribution invaluable—by keeping a file on where those strengths are among your staff, so that when a request comes down from management, you can immediately flag the people most likely to succeed. In whatever way makes sense to your organization, if your HR department can make it happen, you will be making an enormous contribution to your organization's success.

FOR PEOPLE WANTING TO GO ABROAD

Maybe you're reading this book because you are interested in globalizing your own career or are in a field or an organization that is going global and you want to be in on it. Chapters 12 and 13 were dedicated almost entirely to you. But the key advice boils down pretty easily. First, *be honest with yourself*. Take us seriously when we say that not everybody can do this. You may be one of those who can, or you may not. But you owe it to yourself to find out. If you start out in the beginning thinking, "I'm going to go abroad no matter what," you're gambling with your career. You might succeed. But you're far more likely to fail spectacularly, as some of the anecdotes in this book illustrate. You might even get yourself into serious trouble.

This is probably the hardest part. In American and Canadian culture, we're used to thinking that anybody can do anything—that if we just try hard enough and want it enough, we can grow up to be whatever we like. That impulse comes from our broad sense of fairness—you shouldn't be told you can't be a musician just because you were born to the wrong parents. Musical talent can, and frequently does, come from anywhere. But that doesn't mean that *everyone* can be a great musician. The first step here is recognizing this reality: you may be cut out for this, and you may not. Make up your mind now to be honest with yourself.

If you accomplish that, and if you are convinced that you *do* have the qualities to succeed in the international arena, then the rest is relatively straightforward. Do your homework. Get as many experiences as you can with differences—different people, different perspectives, different cultures. Pay attention to differences at all levels—things that don't matter at all to Canadians or

Americans (such as how you hand a business card to someone) might matter a lot to someone else. Learn a language—or more than one. This is where our sense of fairness comes into play, because if you have the right attitudes and the necessary characteristics, then the rest is just a lot of hard work. That's the last thing to learn from the stories we've told here: don't underestimate just how different the rest of the world is, or how many different ways there are to run afoul in it. Nobody masters this quickly or easily. But if you're prepared to work hard at it, it's an exciting road.

CARRY YOUR BUSINESS TO GLOBAL SUCCESS

It should be clear by now that we are enthusiastic backers of globalizing businesses and organizations. So much can be gained by entering into international partnerships. And you can learn many new ways to advance your organization's goals—whether it's selling widgets, educating people, or becoming the best provider of services in your niche. We remain astonished at the number of organizations that won't set foot outside their own country—often, won't even venture beyond their own corner of it.

The kinds of stories we've peppered throughout this book are, of course, part of the explanation. Almost everybody has heard of one or two spectacular failures in the international realm. Sometimes, those failures make the headlines—usually when they're at their most messy, and most costly. That frightens a lot of people. And a lot of organizations may be realistic in thinking, we don't know what we're doing so let's not go abroad.

But we are convinced that circumstances aren't going to allow that kind of thinking for very much longer. A lot of ink has been spilled on globalization, from the condescendingly simple (Thomas Friedman's *The World Is Flat*) to the sophisticated yet readable (Joseph Stiglitz's *Globalization and Its Discontents*). But the underlying realities, as we've mentioned throughout the book, are clear. We are in a period of substantial change and upheaval. This isn't linear change, but paradigm-shifting. (The changes, and the rate of those changes, are tightly linked to an esoteric branch of mathematical physics called *chaos theory*—a theory that is notoriously difficult to understand. So don't feel bad if you find all that is happening around you to be terribly flustering! You're in good company!) The old ways of doing things aren't working anymore. New ways are going to have to be tried. Frequently, those new ways are not found here at home, but overseas—and especially in collaborations that get formed when organizations find good partners abroad.

We'll end this chapter, and this book, where we started. Whatever business you're in—even if you don't think of it as "business"— it's ultimately driven by *people*. People, working together, get things done. Get the right people in the right places, and you can soar to heights you never imagined.

Enjoy the adventure!

Recommended Reading

As with all subjects, there are a ton of books and articles to read on expats, international assignments, and how to achieve success overseas. What we've done here is condense a list of what we consider to be some of the best of that literature. We've grouped it thematically, which will hopefully make the list useful to you.

BUSINESS ADVICE

Although our book covers an area long ignored—how to choose the right people to send overseas—we obviously don't claim to be the final word on all business advice. In writing this book, and in conducting our business, we have consulted a few favorites that we think might be useful to you as well. As you can see, we have a fondness for authors with real-world business experience—stories to tell that can both inspire and instruct. We hope you will find them as useful as we have.

James F. Parker, *Do the Right Thing: How Dedicated Employees Create Loyal Customers and Large Profits* (Upper Saddle River, N.J.: Wharton School Publishing, 2008).
This is not a specifically international business book, but it is so important that it should be on every serious executive's bookshelf. Parker, CEO of Southwest Airlines from 2001 to 2004, tells the story of how his organization not only survived but thrived in the face of the biggest industry catastrophe ever—September 11, 2001. The focus of his book—just like ours—is people. People are what make the organization go—a cliché that everyone mouths, but few enterprises manage to actually get right. If you want to see an example of how a business can throw every rule out the window except one—do the right thing by your people—this is the book for you.

Charles F. Ehret and Lynne Waller Scanlon, *Overcoming Jet Lag* (New York: Berkeley Trade, 1987).
Still the classic in the field, this book is a must-read for anybody troubled by jet lag problems—as well as managers who send people overseas and have trouble understanding why they might not function effectively right away! Ehret's advice throughout is excellent, as is his explanation of jet lag itself.

Chip Conley, *Peak: How Great Companies Get Their Mojo From Maslow* (San Francisco: Jossey-Bass, 2007).
Like Do the Right Thing, *this book isn't specifically international in focus. Also like Parker's book, it tells the story of a CEO—Conley, who started and ran a series of hotel chains—who learned how to be a contrarian, throw out the "usual" rules of business, and focus on* people *as the key to success. Conley uses the psychologist Abraham Maslow's work as the basis for understanding*

how to make a business run far better—and with happier people. Conley's book and Parker's make an excellent set, because they both recognize the same fundamental truth that our book is based on: people are the key to success.

Derek Green, *New World Order: Stories* (Pittsburgh: Autumn House Press, 2008).
Rarely do people in business turn to fiction for advice. But in this case, it is well worth doing. Green, an expat with over twenty years of experience crisscrossing the globe, has put together a collection of short stories about people connected to (fictional) multinational companies, and the kinds of difficulties and troubles they run into. Themes run the gamut from mis-assigned people (a favorite topic of ours!) to cultural misunderstandings, poorly-done cross-cultural training, and the mysteries of other cultural settings often opaque to the Western mind. Well worth reading for managers who have to send people overseas, as well as for the people who are being sent.

John C. Bogle, *Enough. True Measures of Money, Business, and Life* (Hoboken, N.J.: John Wiley & Sons, 2009).
The founder of the most successful mutual fund in America, Bogle practiced his moral principles for decades at Vanguard. This small book defines the powerful concept of "enough," and teaches some other concepts that could easily help turn things around for this country, from markets to family rooms. No wonder it is garnering unprecedented praise from every level of business and society.

Alan C. Greenberg, *Memos from the Chairman* (New York: Workman, 1996).
Ace Greenberg was the venerable chairman of Bear Stearns in the years well ahead of its shameful collapse. In fact, one of us has known him personally for years and attests that if the Ace principles had been practiced after his retirement, Bear Stearns could never have slipped into ignominy. Among these pithy memos of

no-nonsense advice to executives of all ages in business is his holiest rule of all, today ignored by most Americans: return every phone call and return it promptly! *As Ace put it, "I don't care if he's selling malaria—return his call!"*

INTERNATIONAL BUSINESS BLUNDERS

Believe it or not, there is literature devoted just to documenting the amazing mistakes that companies commit when they go overseas. Why write books based on others' mistakes? Because it is hoped they will be instructive. And because, like it or not, we learn better from the mistakes of others than from their successes. A few of the anecdotes in our own book came from such sources, though not many—because there are so many others to choose from, including ours and our colleagues' personal experiences.

Nevertheless, there have been some very good collections of these over the years, and they *are* very instructive reading.

Andrea Mandel-Campbell, *Why Mexicans Don't Drink Molson: Rescuing Canadian Business From the Suds of Global Obscurity* (Vancouver, BC: Douglas & McIntyre, Ltd., 2007).
An extremely well-done book that is aimed at Canadian businesses, we can't recommend it highly enough. And although it focuses on the Canadian market, its stories are likely to be highly instructive to American businesses as well—always better to learn from the mistakes of others! (Somehow Canadians and Americans manage to make the same mistakes over and over again.)

David A. Ricks, et al., *International Business Blunders* (Columbus, OH: Grid, Inc., 1974).
David A. Ricks, *Blunders in International Business* (Oxford, UK/ Malden, MA: Blackwell Publishers, 1999).

Ricks originally put this collection together back in the early 1970s, which goes to show that these problems are not new, and they're not a function of the "globalization" that has been the fashionable buzzword in recent years. He updated the collection in the late 1990s, but many of the original stories still remain. They are just as relevant today as they were nearly forty years ago. Ricks organizes his anecdotes thematically, making these extremely valuable handbooks to have.

Andrew Cohen, *The Unfinished Canadian: The People We Are* (Toronto: McClelland & Stewart, 2007).

Different from Mandel-Campbell's book above in that it offers a panoply of deep thought about what it really means today to be a Canadian. In the process, of course, he makes some indictments of bad business practices, and how Canadians relate to their American neighbors. Given that America is Canada's largest trading partner—and Canada America's—this book has much to teach readers on both sides of the 45th parallel.

ACADEMIC LITERATURE

Scholars at business schools have done a number of studies over the years on the subject of expat success. We cited a few of these studies in chapters of this book, where it made sense to do so. But like most academic literatures, this one is extensive, and much of it is research-oriented, and so takes some translation to convert to real-world business uses. Some of it focuses on questions that are more of interest to scholars than to people in business. Nevertheless, some academic authors have done a good job of working on questions that are of keen interest to businesses sending people overseas. For those looking to get a good overview of the scholarly research on the field, therefore, we recommend the following.

Paula Caligiuri and Wayne Cascio, "*Can We Send Her There? Maximizing the Success of Western Women on Global Assignments,*" *Journal of World Business*, v. 33, n. 4, 1998, pp. 394–416.
Caligiuri has done a lot of research on gender and expatriate success. This article summarizes a lot of research, both hers and others', and so provides a nice overview of the field. If you want a good précis of some of the issues we raised in Chapter 3, this is worth tracking down.

Rosalie Tung, "Do Race and Gender Matter in International Assignments To/From Asia Pacific?" *Human Resource Management*, v. 47, n. 1, Spring 2008, pp. 91–110.
Like Caligiuri, Tung has done a great deal of research on expatriate success. We cited some of her work in earlier chapters. In this piece, Tung adds the dimension of race, and looks particularly at the Asia-Pacific region, where race and gender have interesting interactions.

Rita Bennett, Anne Aston, and Tracy Colquhoun, "Cross-Cultural Training: A Critical Step in Ensuring the Success of International Assignments," *Human Resource Management*, v. 39, nos. 2–3, Summer/Fall 2000, pp. 239–250.
Remarkably, as we point out in the book, many companies don't do much cross-cultural training, and some do none at all. This article is both a good argument for why companies should make this a part of their game plan, and a good overview of major components that should be included.

Bibliography

Aycan, Zeynep. "Expatriate adjustment as a multifaceted phenomenon: Individual and organizational level predictors." *International Journal of Human Resource Management* 8, no. 4 (1997): 434–56.

Beaman, Karen V. "Myths, Mystiques, and Mistakes in Overseas Assignments: The Role of Global Mindset in International Work." *IHRIM Journal*, November/December 2004, 40–53.

Bennett, Rita, Anne Aston, and Tracy Colquhoun. "Cross-Cultural Training: A Critical Step in Ensuring the Success of International Assignments." *Human Resource Management* 39 (2000): 239–50.

Brafman, Ori and Rom Brafman. *Sway: The Irresistible Pull of Irrational Behavior.* New York: Doubleday, 2008.

Caligiuri, Paula and Wayne Cascio. *"Can We Send Her There?* Maximizing the Success of Western Women on Global Assignments." *Journal of World Business* 33, no. 4 (1998): 394–416.

Caligiuri, Paula and Jean Phillips. "An application of self-assessment realistic job previews to expatriate assignments." *International*

Journal of Human Resource Management 14, no. 7 (2003): 1102–16.

Caligiuri, Paula and Rosalie Tung. "Comparing the success of male and female expatriates from a US-based multinational company." *International Journal of Human Resource Management* 10, no. 5 (1999): 763–82.

Cohen, Andrew. *The Unfinished Canadian: The People We Are*. Toronto: Emblem Editions, 2007.

Dinges, Norman G. and Kathleen D. Baldwin. "Intercultural Competence: A Research Perspective." In *Handbook of Intercultural Training*, 2nd ed., eds, Dan Landis and Rabi Bhagat, 106–23. Thousand Oaks, CA: Sage, 1996.

Drew, Pat. "Overseas Assignments: A Team Approach to Selecting the Right Candidate." *Innovations in International HR*, Summer 2008, http://www.patdrew.org/docs/Innovations_overseas_2008.pdf.

Ehret, Charles. *Overcoming Jet Lag*. (Berkeley: Berkeley Trade, 1987).

Ewers, Justin. "Taking a Foreign Flier: In the global age, an overseas assignment could be just the answer for your resume." *US News & World Report*, March 12, 2006, http://www.usnews.com/usnews/biztech/articles/060320/20overseas_print.htm.

"Expatriation: The Toughest Test." *Healthcare International*, October 2008, http://www.healthcare-int.com/expatriate-workers.html.

"Globetrotters '08." *Human Resources Magazine*, June 10, 2008, http://www.humanresourcesmagazine.com.au/articles/74/0C057174.asp?Type=60&Category=882.

Harvey, Michale and Milorad Novicevic. "Selecting expatriates for increasingly complex global assignments." *Career Development International* 6, no. 2 (2001): 69–86.

Hayes, Cassandra. "The intrigue of international assignments: If you're prepared, career advancement, leadership opportunity and a diversified experience can be yours." *Black Enterprise* 26, no. 10 (1996): 98–102.

Heuser, Achim. "Foreign assignments: Weighing up pros and cons." *IHK WirkschaftsForum*, November 2003, 44–45.

Hutton, John. *The World of the International Manager.* Atlantic Highlands, NJ: Humanities Press, 1988.

"Is an Expatriate Assignment for You?" *International Business Center Newsletter*, October 2008, http://www.international-business-center .com/international_newsletter/volume2_issue4.htm.

Kealey, Daniel J. "The Challenge of International Personnel Selection." In *Handbook of Intercultural Training*, ed. Daniel Landis, Janet Bennett, and Milton Bennett, 81–105. Thousand Oaks, CA: Sage, 1996.

Lall, Sohan "Billy". "Gender Bias and the Foreign Client." *Online Ethics Center for Engineering*, August 7, 2006, http://www.onlineethics .org/CMS/workplacediv/divmiscproblems/slclient.aspx.

Lowe, Kevin, Meredith Downes, and K. Galen Kroeck. "The Impact of Gender and Location on the Willingness to Accept Overseas Assignments." *International Journal of Human Resource Management* 10, no. 2 (1999): 223–34.

Mandel-Campbell, Andrea. *Why Mexicans Don't Drink Molson: Rescuing Canadian Business from the Suds of Global Obscurity.* Vancouver, BC: Douglas & McIntyre, 2007.

Meckman, Saskia. "What Is Really Being Done? Maximizing the Success of Women on Overseas Assignments." *Expatrium*, March 2002, http://www.expatexchange.com/lib.cfm?articleID=937.

O'Hara-Devereaux, Mary and Robert Johansen. *Globalwork: Bridging Distance, Culture, and Time.* San Francisco: Jossey-Bass, 1994.

Parker, James F. *Do the Right Thing: How Dedicated Employees Create Loyal Customers and Large Profits.* Upper Saddle River, NJ: Wharton School Publishing, 2007.

Quelch, John A. and Helen Bloom. "Ten Steps to a Global Human Resource Strategy." In *Best Practices in International Business*, ed. Michael Czinkota and Ilkka Ronkainen, 207–20. Forth Worth, TX: Harcourt College Publishers, 2000.

Reeves, Scott. "Saying Sayonara to Travel Faux Pas." *Forbes*, July 27, 2005, http://www.forbes.com/2005/07/27/career-travel-etiquette-cx_ sr_0728bizbasics.html?partner=daily_newsletter.

Ricks, David. *Blunders in International Business.* Oxford: Blackwell, 1999.

Ricks, David et al. *International Business Blunders.* Columbus, OH: Grid, 1974.

Selmer, Jan and Hon Lam. "Using Former 'Third Culture Kids' as a Recruitment Source for Business Expatriates with Success Potential." *BRC Papers of Cross-Cultural Management,* 2002, 1–24.

Shaffer, Margaret A. et al. "You Can Take It with You: Individual Differences and Expatriate Effectiveness." *BRC Papers of Cross-Cultural Management,* 2005, 1–35.

Stolz, Richard F. "Worldly Wise." *Human Resource Executive Online,* November 1, 2004, http://www.hreonline.com/HRE/printstory.jsp?storyId=4222869.

Trompenaars, Fons and Charles Hampden-Turner. *Riding the Waves of Culture: Understanding Cultural Diversity in Global Business.* 2nd ed. New York: McGraw-Hill, 1997.

Tung, Rosalie. "Do Race and Gender Matter in International Assignments to/from Asia Pacific?" *Human Resource Management* 47, no. 1 (2008): 91–110.

Tzeng, Rueyling. "Gender Issues and Family Concerns for Women with International Careers: Female Expatriates in Western Multinational Corporations in Taiwan." *Women in Management Review* 21, no. 5 (2006): 376–92.

Time Zone Planning:
A Handy Tool

As we mentioned in Chapter 6, managing across time zones can be very difficult for the uninitiated. Unless you have a natural talent for it, you may find it difficult to do time-zone conversions in your head. Say you're trying to plan a teleconference between people in your home office in New York and your branch office in Berlin. When should the meeting be?

We've found that the best tool for managing these kinds of differences has already been put together by a Norwegian programmer named Steffen Thorsen, who back in the 1990s put together a small company called Time and Date AS. His Web site, www.timeanddate.com, is full of useful tools and tips. One of the best is his World Clock Meeting Planner, www.timeanddate.com/worldclock/meeting.html. It allows you to enter up to four different cities (other tools on the Web site will go up to six), and creates an easy-to-read graphical readout to show when overlaps exist during normal business hours (the light gray zones below), when you might stretch for an early morning or evening (white), and what times are generally off-limits (dark gray). A planner for a NY-Berlin meeting would look like this:

UTC time	New York	Berlin
Thursday, January 14, 2010 at 23:00:00	Thu 6:00 PM	Midnight Thu-Fri
Friday, January 15, 2010 at 00:00:00	Thu 7:00 PM	Fri 1:00 AM
Friday, January 15, 2010 at 01:00:00	Thu 8:00 PM	Fri 2:00 AM
Friday, January 15, 2010 at 02:00:00	Thu 9:00 PM	Fri 3:00 AM
Friday, January 15, 2010 at 03:00:00	Thu 10:00 PM	Fri 4:00 AM
Friday, January 15, 2010 at 04:00:00	Thu 11:00 PM	Fri 5:00 AM
Friday, January 15, 2010 at 05:00:00	Midnight Thu-Fri	Fri 6:00 AM
Friday, January 15, 2010 at 06:00:00	Fri 1:00 AM	Fri 7:00 AM
Friday, January 15, 2010 at 07:00:00	Fri 2:00 AM	Fri 8:00 AM
Friday, January 15, 2010 at 08:00:00	Fri 3:00 AM	Fri 9:00 AM
Friday, January 15, 2010 at 09:00:00	Fri 4:00 AM	Fri 10:00 AM
Friday, January 15, 2010 at 10:00:00	Fri 5:00 AM	Fri 11:00 AM
Friday, January 15, 2010 at 11:00:00	Fri 6:00 AM	Fri 12:00 Noon
Friday, January 15, 2010 at 12:00:00	Fri 7:00 AM	Fri 1:00 PM
Friday, January 15, 2010 at 13:00:00	Fri 8:00 AM	Fri 2:00 PM
Friday, January 15, 2010 at 14:00:00	Fri 9:00 AM	Fri 3:00 PM
Friday, January 15, 2010 at 15:00:00	Fri 10:00 AM	Fri 4:00 PM
Friday, January 15, 2010 at 16:00:00	Fri 11:00 AM	Fri 5:00 PM
Friday, January 15, 2010 at 17:00:00	Fri 12:00 Noon	Fri 6:00 PM
Friday, January 15, 2010 at 18:00:00	Fri 1:00 PM	Fri 7:00 PM
Friday, January 15, 2010 at 19:00:00	Fri 2:00 PM	Fri 8:00 PM
Friday, January 15, 2010 at 20:00:00	Fri 3:00 PM	Fri 9:00 PM
Friday, January 15, 2010 at 21:00:00	Fri 4:00 PM	Fri 10:00 PM
Friday, January 15, 2010 at 22:00:00	Fri 5:00 PM	Fri 11:00 PM
Friday, January 15, 2010 at 23:00:00	Fri 6:00 PM	Midnight Fri-Sat
Saturday, January 16, 2010 at 00:00:00	Fri 7:00 PM	Sat 1:00 AM
Saturday, January 16, 2010 at 01:00:00	Fri 8:00 PM	Sat 2:00 AM
Saturday, January 16, 2010 at 02:00:00	Fri 9:00 PM	Sat 3:00 AM
Saturday, January 16, 2010 at 03:00:00	Fri 10:00 PM	Sat 4:00 AM
Saturday, January 16, 2010 at 04:00:00	Fri 11:00 PM	Sat 5:00 AM

☐ NORMAL BUSINESS HOURS
☐ EARLY MORNING/EVENING HOURS
▨ NON-WORKING HOURS

12-Hour and 24-Hour Time Conversions

12-Hour Time	24-Hour Time
1:00 AM	01:00
2:00 AM	02:00
3:00 AM	03:00
4:00 AM	04:00
5:00 AM	05:00
6:00 AM	06:00
7:00 AM	07:00
8:00 AM	08:00
9:00 AM	09:00
10:00 AM	10:00
11:00 AM	11:00
12:00 NOON	12:00
1:00 PM	13:00
2:00 PM	14:00
3:00 PM	15:00
4:00 PM	16:00
5:00 PM	17:00
6:00 PM	18:00
7:00 PM	19:00
8:00 PM	20:00
9:00 PM	21:00
10:00 PM	22:00
11:00 PM	23:00
12:00 MIDNIGHT	24:00

A Few Useful Language Phrases

Phrase	German	French	Spanish	Russian	Turkish
Yes	Ja (ya)	Ouí (WEE)	Sí (SEE)	Да (DAH)	Evet (eh-VET)
No	Nein (nine)	Non (naw)	No	Нет (NYET)	Hayır (HIGH-er)
Hello	Guten tag (GOOT-en TOG)	Bonjour (bong-ZHOOR)	Hola (OH-lah)	Здравствуйте (ZDRAVST-vweet-yeh)	Merhaba (MEHR-hah-bah)
Good	Gut (GOOT)	Bien (bee-YEN)	Bueno (BWAY-no)	Хорошо (khoro-SHOW)	İyi (ee-yee)
Thank you	Danke (DONK-eh)	Merci (mehr-SEE)	Gracias (GRAH-see-ahs)	Спасибо (spah-SEE-boh)	Teşekkürler (tesh-eh-KIER-lehr)
Thank you very much	Vielen Dank (FEEL-en DONK)	Merci beaucoup (mehr-SEE boh-KOO)	Muchas gracias (MOO-chahs GRAH-see-ahs)	Большое спасибо (bal'-SHOW-yeh spah-SEE-boh)	Çok teşekkürler (choke tesh-eh-KIER-lehr)
Thank you for your time	Danke für Ihre Zeit. (DONK-eh fuehr IRR-eh-TZITE)	Merci pour votre temps. (mehr-SEE poor VOTE-reh TOMP)	Gracias por su tiempo. (GRAH-see-ahs por soo tee-YEM-poh)	Спасибо за ваше время. (spah-SEE-boh za vash-eh VREM-ya)	Mersi için senin zaman. (mehr-SEE ee-cheen sen-EEN zah-MAHN)
You're welcome	Bitte (BIT-teh)	De riens (duh ree-ENH)	De nada (day NAH-dah)	Не за что (NYEH-za-shto)	Bir şey değil (beer shay deh-EEL)
Please	Bitte (BIT-teh)	S'il vous plait (SEE voo PLAY)	Por favor (por fah-VOR)	Пожалуйста (po-ZHAL'-sta)	Lütfen (LYOOT-fen)
I understand	Ich verstehe. (ish fer-SHTAYH-uh)	Je comprend. (zhuh kom-PRAWN)	Entiendo. (eyn-tee-YEN-doh)	Понимаю. (pon-ee-MY-yoo)	Anliyorum. (ahn-lee-YOR-oom)
I don't understand	Ich verstehe nicht. (ish fer-SHTAYH-uh nisht)	Je ne comprend pas. (zhuh nuh kom-prawn PAH)	No entiendo. (no eyn-tee-YEN-doh)	Не понимаю. (NEE pon-ee-MY-yoo)	Anlamıyorum. (ahn-lahm-ee-YOR-oom)
Excuse me	Entschuldigung! (ent-SHOOL-dih-goong)	Excusez-moi. (ex-KYOO-zay mwah)	Perdóneme. (pehr-DOH-nay-may)	Извините! (eez-ven-EE-tyeh)	Afedersiniz! (ah-feh-DEHR-sin-eez)
I'm sorry	Es tut mir Leid. (ehs toot meer LIGHT)	Je suis désolé. (zhuh swee DAY-so-LAY)	Lo siento. (low see-YEN-toh)	Я сожалею. (ya sozh-al-YAY-yoo)	Üzgünüm. (OOZ-goon-nyoom)
Pleased to meet you	Es freut mich! (ehs FROYT mish)	Enchanté! (on-shawn-TAY)	Muy encantado! (moo-ee en-con-TAH-doh)	Очень приятно Вас познакомиться! (OH-chun Pree-YAHT-no vahs poz-na-KOH-mit-suh)	Çok memnun oldum! (choke mem-NOON ol-DOOM)

Index

About the Authors

BRUCE ALAN JOHNSON

Mr. Johnson has run his own businesses worldwide since 1985. His company, Bruce Alan Johnson Associates, helps clients in a number of countries tackle international problems. Having lived off and on in Africa, Europe, and elsewhere overseas for over thirty years, Johnson began teaching entrepreneurism to South African blacks in 1978, then was arrested and banned from South Africa by the government in 1979, only to be readmitted and granted a residency visa after the lifting of *apartheid*.

A *cum laude* graduate of Claremont Men's College, Mr. Johnson teaches occasionally in an adjunct capacity and writes in the areas of Philosophy, International Relations, the Effective Use of Interdisciplinary Thinking, and the History of Ideas. He is also recognized as a world expert on avian influenza, or bird flu.

Mr. Johnson has traveled in seventy-six countries over the past forty-one years and lived in Europe, Turkey, and Africa. He is fluent in German, Russian, Spanish, and Turkish; conversant in French, Bulgarian, Afrikaans, and Swahili, and reads Greek and Latin. He is a former senior U.S. intelligence officer, having worked for a number of years with non-American intelligence organizations on special projects in the Middle East and the former Soviet bloc.

Aside from having served part-time in the White House in 1985-88, his former positions include senior fellow for the Hudson Institute (a leading world think tank); vice president of Worldwide Affairs for Hill & Knowlton (the world's largest public relations firm); director of Business Development for ITT-Telecommunications; director of International Marketing & Operations for Schlumberger's data communications division Rixon (a leading French petro-technology firm); and manager of International Marketing for RACAL (the British electronics and telecommunications conglomerate).

He has served as a director on the board of the Washington International Trade Association. Formerly international editor for a leading radio publication, *QST*, Mr. Johnson writes regularly for newspapers and journals around the world. His work has appeared in more than seventy-eight countries, most recently in *Reader's Digest, The Freeman, Telecommunications,* and the *Wall Street Journal.*

Mr. Johnson has served as a delegate for the U.S. government in global telecommunications conferences in Nairobi and Geneva; as special adviser to the president of the Republic of Bulgaria, the Hon. Dr. Zhelyu Zhelev; and was nominated in 1992 by *Inc.* magazine as Entrepreneur of the Year.

R. WILLIAM AYRES

Dr. Ayres has a career spanning a dozen years as a university professor and administrator. A scholar of international conflict, identity politics, and foreign policy, Dr. Ayres has published widely in both professional and popular outlets. Dr. Ayres's scholarly research on identity politics, international conflict and conflict resolution, and American foreign policy has been published in several peer-reviewed journals and edited books. He has also penned dozens of opinion articles and papers for local and national outlets as disparate as *USA Today* and *The Progressive Christian*. He has given numerous TV and radio interviews on politics and foreign policy, and hosted a current events radio show, "News and Views," on WICR 88.7 FM in Indianapolis for two years.

During his academic career on the faculties of four different colleges and universities, Dr. Ayres has worked extensively on programs of international education and bridge-building. He has traveled professionally to many countries, including Austria, Cyprus, Canada, Switzerland, Great Britain, and South Africa. He developed international exchange and cooperation programs between universities in the United States and South Africa, and negotiated partnerships with campuses on Cyprus and in Athens, Greece. He served as a political consultant to one of the major political parties in the South African parliament, where his research has been featured in parliamentary debate. He is today examining the ever-widening impact of international business on world events, and on how simpler scenario thinking might alleviate some business difficulties.

Dr. Ayres received his BA in Political Science from Williams College, where he graduated *magna cum laude* and was elected to Phi Beta Kappa. He went on to earn his master's and doctoral degrees, also in Political Science, at The Ohio State University. In his teaching career, Dr. Ayres has taught a broad range of courses to hundreds of undergraduate and graduate students, on international topics spanning the fields of history, geography, psychology, and political science, and including courses on negotiation, mediation, nationalism, foreign policy, and global interdependence. He has given guest lectures and keynote addresses at dozens of conferences and events, with audiences ranging from undergraduate students to CEOs and high-level corporate managers.

Author Contact Information

The authors are available to assist with issues related to this book, and to help American and Canadian organizations with problems in the international area. We can best be reached through our company, Bruce Alan Johnson Associates:

Web site: *www.bajassociates.com*
Bruce e-mail: baj@bajassociates.com
Bruce cell: +1-802-323-3834
Bill e-mail: rwa@bajassociates.com
Bill cell: +1-717-449-1150